CASE METHOD^{SM}

Business Interviewing

About the Authors

Dr Linda Hickman was born and raised in the United States and lived for many years in Palo Alto, California. She received her bachelor's and master's degrees from Stanford University and her doctorate from Ohio State University. Her graduate work was in the field of international planning and development which led to a career with academic posts and consulting in over sixteen countries. In 1988, she came to London as a visiting faculty member for an overseas programme in international business, and shortly afterwards joined Oracle Corporation UK as a Corporate Consultant.

At Oracle Corporation UK, Linda contributes to defining structured methods in the area of strategic development at the enterprise level. The techniques she uses for interviewing have been developed and refined during her twenty-year consulting career which spans fifteen industries with clients in public and private organizations across the globe. Linda served Oracle Europe as a consultancy manager for Central and East European countries and was responsible for all consultancy, training and support for staff and clients, with many projects based on CASE tools and CASE Method. She is frequently invited to lecture on strategic business systems development, expert systems, CASE and her current work in business process re-engineering.

Linda lives in London with her daughter Michelle. Her other two grown children, Sasha and Jeffrey, are beginning their own careers in California.

Cliff Longman was born in Harrow, England, in 1959. He attended Lanchester Polytechnic, where he received his degree in Computer Science.

He spent the early part of his career designing database and realtime systems in the manufacturing, travel and communications industries. After two years working in Europe, he joined Oracle as a consultant, where he helped to develop the training and education services for the Company. In his role of Corporate Consultant, Cliff has led analysis teams on some of the largest strategic studies undertaken by Oracle. He later joined the CASE Product Development Group, where he helps to develop CASE Method and acts as the chief architect for the computer tools to support it.

Cliff is married with two children and lives in Surrey, England.

Linda and Cliff have worked together as corporate consultants, training, consulting and developing methods and techniques over a period of nearly six years.

CASE METHOD[SM]

Business Interviewing

LINDA HICKMAN
CLIFF LONGMAN

 Addison-Wesley Publishing Company

Wokingham, England • Reading, Massachusetts • Menlo Park, California
New York • Don Mills, Ontario • Amsterdam • Bonn • Sydney • Singapore
Tokyo • Madrid • San Juan • Milan • Paris • Mexico City • Seoul • Taipei

ORACLE®

The Relational Database Management System

The book was produced using Ventura Publisher and CorelDRAW.
Cover designed by Hybert Design & Type, Maidenhead.
Printed in The United States of America.

First printed 1994.

Written by Linda Hickman and Cliff Longman.
Edited and illustrated by Barbara Barker, with cartoons by Paul Williams.

ISBN 0-201-59372-6

British Library Cataloguing in Publication Data
A catalogue record for this book is available from the British Library.

Library of Congress Cataloging in Publication Data is available.

Other books available in the CASE Method series:
   Tasks and Deliverables
   Entity Relationship Modelling
   Function and Process Modelling
   Fast-track: A RAD Approach

When ordering this book through Oracle Corporation please quote the Part Number A23446. Contact:

Oracle Corporation UK Ltd	World Headquarters
The Oracle Centre	Oracle Corporation
The Ring, Bracknell	500 Oracle Parkway
Berkshire, RG12 1BW	Redwood Shores, CA 94065
UK	USA

DEDICATION

To my father: a wise teacher who taught me to actively question and listen.

Linda

To my family: the most precious thing in my life with whom I discovered the real benefit of open questions.

Cliff

FOREWORD

Why a book about interviewing? And for that matter why interviewing in a business context? If we need a new business process, can I, as head of my department, not just sit down at my desk and define the new process? It is, after all, my responsibility; my department; my head on the block if it goes wrong. Surely I know best what is needed? Look at the advantages of this approach: I get quick results; unproductive debate is curtailed; I can implement it *carte blanche* on Monday.

In the computer industry we tend to feel we can ignore interviewing. We are the obvious custodians of high technology. We know about Terabytes of storage, information superhighways, the Internet, multi-media and object-oriented programming. Creating a new order processing, personnel or manufacturing system is no problem. *"Just give me my machine and the latest GUI development tools. What they really need is a video widget in the top corner, a sound icon down here, an OLE link for when they use spreadsheets, a bit of database independence for when the business switches from relational to object database, a speech-recognition input system (so I can experiment with cross-language automatic translation)."*

Familiar? The undisciplined management approach of starting a journey before determining the destination. And the technocrat know-all who believes that your insurance company, chemical plant, government department or business is there purely for his amusement. But the most successful people in industry and government are the tiny minority who have insight and a clear vision of what is needed. And the most successful businesses are those that can harness the insight of the few, along with the pragmatism and experience of others to really understand what is needed before change is initiated. What is needed for a business does not come out of books and paper documentation. It comes out of the heads of a small number of people who collectively **know** what is needed but have not necessarily been able to articulate it. The interviewer's job is to get to that essence, with indications of how it might be achieved, what obstacles must be removed and then work with some form of designer to synthesize a model of what is needed in the future. The model may take different forms to enable the instigators to visualize the intent, verify or correct the model, check the concept and then go on to a successful implementation.

Having established the need for interviewing, discussion, group data-gathering sessions or other form of knowledge elicitation, it is vital you have competence in the skill of interviewing. The primary deliverable from any interview is a note of useful ideas, facts and other things that come to mind (from **any** source) during the discussion. Learn how to take notes – without that skill brilliant insights can be lost forever. An analogy might be dreaming. During the last few moments before waking your mind is whirling around topics and you suddenly solve that critical problem. Success is assured. You confidently wake up and ...

The second thing is to **survive**. This may sound melodramatic but many a promising career has been stalled by a single meeting or a misplaced word. You may survive; your project may not. Politics is rife in any business and if you are unaware of side issues your interviewee may take the opportunity to expedite a hidden agenda. Survival requires planning, care, human interaction skills and the ability to gently (or occasionally firmly) steer the discussion towards better purposes. A useful approach is to be apolitical, to ask interesting and penetrating questions, to be genuinely interested, professional and reactive about new insights gained. You may need to be persistent, letting the hidden agenda run its course before your interviewee relaxes and allows you to pursue your goals.

Too much interviewing can become boring for you – the interviewer or note-taker. It is important to interview the smallest number of people that, in combination, understand what is needed. This enables the drivers of the interviews to enjoy their role, be enthusiastic and proactively become part of the business – an ally to the interviewee. With this synergy startling results can occur which may move your project forward dramatically, help the business and even draw the comment from a top executive: *"That was excellent; probably the first time I really understood our business."*

Interviewing, like any other skill, has to be learned. There are many pit-falls and this book comes from years of practical experience, balanced by associated academic theory. To become proficient, read, practise and review, so that when you next get asked to re-engineer a process or build a system it can be based on what is really needed, not on individual whim.

Richard Barker
Senior Vice President, OpenVision

PREFACE

In our consultancy role, we find that interviews play a major part in the information gathering for any project. We have learned that the activity is a valuable opportunity for discovering many layers of information. Where we once looked on it as a data collection activity, now we consider it one that can provide real knowledge and understanding of the individuals we are interviewing.

We enjoy interviewing and have become more and more fascinated with the whole process of communication. We find ourselves interviewing in varied industries, countries and cultures. In such situations, we are looking at how we can best create an environment for a free interchange of ideas and be able to interpret accurately the information we gather. The last part is the most difficult. Semantics and differing sets of assumptions blur our view of what we have heard. Throughout any interview, we are trying to put aside our own preconceptions and listen with an open mind. It is not easy. The task is made easier, however, by having a set of techniques in hand for interviewing.

The mechanics of an interview are just that, mechanisms for smoothing a process. Once the interview process can be carried out with less effort, we can devote our time and attention to the real issues that are being discussed. That is why we are focusing in this book on the techniques for interviewing – on **how** to interview – with the goal of helping you have more time to concentrate on the real part of the interview – on **what** is actually being said.

Over the years we have come to value the practical techniques we have discovered which enable us to get below the surface in an interview to really understand the perspective of the interviewee. We believe that

Information Technology practitioners in particular have an opportunity to improve their knowledge and understanding of what the needs of their business are and thus to dramatically improve the role they play in their business. Good interviewing techniques become an important asset.

The understanding we gain from an interview brings with it another challenge. We must often take the information from one interview and combine it with results from several other interviews in order to build a picture, or models, about our understanding. At that point, clarifying meaning becomes especially critical. It is the dilemma of converging various points of view that brings us closest to the real issue in an interview – understanding what is being said. We have been developing techniques to help us with that task and want to share them with others.

A book develops slowly. Several years ago Linda wrote some practical guidelines for interviewing. We used feedback from practitioners to expand the guidelines, which in turn formed the starting point for this book. We hope that this book will help to answer more questions and lead to rewarding and successful interviews.

To all new and experienced interviewers alike – good luck.

Acknowledgements

The book evolved slowly and with the invaluable assistance of many people. We would like to thank a few personally, and hope that all the other special people who have influenced our ideas and development of the book will know who they are, too. In particular, Jeanette Longman spent many long hours patiently setting up material and resetting it; Barbara Barker has the genius to take all the parts and put them together in a readable, attractive book; Paul Williams has an artistic eye and enlivened the text; Richard Barker, as the originator of CASE Method, has a special role which cannot be measured.

Others also contributed along the way. Sue Ladbrook daily helps keep Linda's schedule manageable in countless ways, and among associates who read carefully and encouraged more interview materials were Renée Taylor and Jeremy Davis. Countless colleagues in projects in many countries over the years have contributed to our understanding of interviewing.

Finally, a big thank you to our understanding families who have enthusiastically supported the idea of the book.

Linda Hickman and Cliff Longman
November 1994

CONTENTS

Appendices

Chapter

1

INTRODUCTION

How do you gather facts, figures and opinions – for a business project? for the requirements of an information system? for a client assignment? Interviews are a significant source of this information. Ensuring a successful interview, however, involves more than goodwill and communication skills – it requires the application of specific techniques, before, during and after the event.

Systems analysts, knowledge engineers, project managers, management consultants, business students and many other professionals, including architects, lawyers and doctors, may use interviewing to gather information in the course of their work activities.

An interview is a conversation where one person aims to understand the other person's knowledge of a subject. Through interviewing, experience acquired by business managers, experts and opinion leaders can be made available to you and your project team. An interview can be seen as a conversation with clear objectives and scope, requiring a degree of preparation, but otherwise similar to a conversation you might have with a friend or a member of the family.

Interviewing turns out to be more than just a way of passing on knowledge of a topic. It is an important mechanism for involving participants in a project. It is a means of the interviewee contributing experience, ideas and concerns, as well as feeling confident that his or her contribution has been heard and taken into consideration. This important aspect of interviewing – actively involving people in a project – can significantly improve the chances of a project's success.

Materials collected during one or more interviews, mostly in the form of notes, may be used as direct input to a structured modelling exercise, so that models can be used to check the consistency and completeness of the information gained. Other books in the CASE Method series concentrate on specific business modelling techniques, such as function and process modelling and entity relationship modelling.

Objectives of Interviewing

The main objectives of an information gathering interview are to:

- discover information being sought from the interviewee accurately and efficiently
- record this information so that it may be easily used as input to the next step in a project (for example, as input to a structured modelling exercise)
- leave the interviewee confident that his/her understanding of the topic has been explored, listened to and valued.

The Interview Process

Planning and Preparation

One of the main differences between a casual conversation and an interview is the degree of planning and preparation required. An interview is for a specific purpose and needs to have clear aims and objectives if it is to be efficient. A well-prepared interviewer will have prepared questions, acquired background knowledge of the subject matter and organized the environment (such as room, seating and refreshments) in order to carry off a short, but intense, information-collection exercise successfully.

Conducting an Interview

The two major roles in conducting an interview are interviewer and note-taker. These require various skills to be practised effectively. For the interviewer, the key skills are the ability to converse in a professional business context and mastery of a selection of questioning techniques, with the ability to apply them appropriately in various circumstances. For the note-taker, accurate note-taking with the ability to analyze what is being said without imposing subjective ideas, prejudices and feelings on the subject is key.

Using the Information Gained

Once an interview has finished, the material collected must be used effectively. In a system development project, this may mean consolidating notes and producing structured models that reflect the contributions of a number of interviewees. In a business project, such as a Business Process Re-engineering exercise, this may mean adding ideas for improvement to a list of issues and problems about the way a process currently works. It is important to know what you are going to do with the information from an interview before you start the interview.

Major Deliverables

From interviews where the primary goal is to collect information in a system development context, the major deliverables fall into two categories:

- tangible deliverables:
  - your notes, consolidated and perhaps converted into a structured form
  - copies of relevant documents to read
  - references to other sources of information

- the intangibles
  - a better understanding of the subject matter
  - increased commitment to the project being carried out
  - and for the interviewee, a sense of genuine contribution to the project and confidence in the project team.

Key Factors

Figure 1-1
Key Factors

Key factors that influence the success of an interview are:

- Interview Objectives
- Information Gathering
- Business Relevance
- Attitude
- Involvement
- Interviewing the Right People
- Perception and Fact

Interview Objectives

Setting clear objectives for each interview is perhaps the most important aspect of preparation that can be done. Without clear objectives, what will provide a focus? How will you know if the interview was successful?

Information Gathering

The interviewing techniques in this book are dedicated to gathering information. As an interviewing team, you should keep the purpose of an interview in mind at all times and use it as a guide for collecting information at the right level of detail.

Business Relevance

It is all too easy for information system developers to lapse into detailed questioning about what a computer system should do. This book intentionally ignores the computer system and focuses on interviewing business people about what they know and understand best – business issues. We make no apologies for this – it is our belief that computer professionals can come up with good technical designs for a system so long as they understand what the business needs really are, so we have dedicated this book solely to that purpose.

Attitude

If you have ever talked to someone who was not interested in what you were saying, or itching to get away for some other reason, you will appreciate why we say that the attitude of the interview team is a key factor! Each interview should be conducted with enthusiasm, genuine interest and a sense of purpose that leaves the interviewee in no doubt of the value you place on his or her contribution. Inquisitive people naturally make good interviewers because they always try to understand in depth what is being said. Each interview should incorporate this inquisitiveness, conducted professionally and with courtesy towards the interviewee.

Involvement

A good interview pays back something to the interviewee in return for contributing information. This can simply be the opportunity to make a contribution and feel that it has been genuinely listened to and considered; or it may be possible to add significantly to the interviewee's understanding of an area that he or she does not know so much about. Such a payback not only justifies the interviewee spending the time, but also reinforces positive commitment to a project. By the questions they ask, experienced interviewers help their interviewees to understand about areas related to their businesses.

Interviewing the Right People

The choice of people to interview in a project is critical. Too many interviews will raise costs beyond what is necessary or economic; too few may mean insufficient coverage of the scope of a project; and choosing the wrong people to interview can produce biased, skewed or inaccurate information. The selection of interviewees is dealt with in Chapter 5 on Preparation.

Perception and Fact

Throughout the interview process it is important to distinguish between perception and fact. Your interviewees can only tell you about the way they perceive the world. Two people may perceive the same facts very differently.

Context for Interviewing

What sort of project needs interviews? How big must a project be to warrant formal interviews? How many interviews are appropriate?

This book focuses on information-gathering interviews as part of a business system development exercise. It assumes that there is a community of business people, with needs for information about their business, and a community of computer professionals capable of providing information systems that satisfy those needs. Unfortunately, the computer professional often does not know what the business person **really** needs. Interviewing can solve this problem.

Although business information gathering is the primary focus of the book, we believe that the techniques presented here are applicable to a wide range of business situations and do not, for example, require information systems to be developed following an interview programme. Whenever it is valuable to pass on information and understanding, an interview can be considered an appropriate vehicle for the transfer, but the degree of formality and scale should be adjusted appropriately. Whether you are a professional, like the architect in our case study seeking client requirements and specifications, or a knowledge engineer, perhaps working to produce a small system to assist an expert in a family legal practice, or you have the task of re-engineering the global operations of a major oil company, interviewing can play a part.

How to Use This Book

This book is designed to give the novice insight into and understanding of the interviewing process and to provide more experienced and expert interviewers with advanced techniques and useful guidelines. It is divided into three main parts, each applicable to an audience with different experience.

The continuing story of the fictitious airline Atlantis Island Flights, which is about to expand into the hotel business, is used as the main case study throughout the book. We follow the initial round of interviews, drawing upon various points in the hotel project. A brief history of this project and some of its main players can be found in Appendix A, "The Story of a Project".

Introducing Interviewing

Chapters 2 to 4 introduce interviewing to the novice. There are no pre-requisites and if you are new to the whole subject this is the place to start. We set the scene in Chapter 2 with a simple example of an interview, from early in the Atlantis project. This is analyzed in Chapter 3, which covers the basic skills needed for interviewing at an outline level, and Chapter 4 suggests some ways to try out and practise these newly discovered techniques.

Basic Techniques

Chapters 5 to 8 go into some depth on each topic introduced in Chapters 2 to 4. If you have been involved in interviewing before, but have not been formally taught the techniques, this section of the book will provide a detailed reference to the basic principles of interviewing. Once the novice has 'consumed' the introductory chapters and tried some of the techniques, Chapters 5 to 8 will help to consolidate the learning.

Advanced Techniques   Chapters 9 to 11 are for the experienced interviewer, covering advanced topics such as non-verbal communication and adapting your techniques to the stage of a business system life cycle. And for those of you who want to know more, we have provided a list for further reading.

For Other Readers   Project managers will find Chapter 5, "Interview Preparation", and Chapter 11, "Interviewing in a Business System Life Cycle", of primary interest and managers in general should find Chapter 3 useful.

Guide to Using the Book

Part of book	Chapter — Type of reader	Novice	Inter-mediate	Expert	Project Manager	Manager
	1 Introduction	✓	✓	✓	✓	✓
Introducing Interviewing	2 A Simple Example	✓	review			
	3 Basic Interviewing	✓	review		✓	✓
	4 Getting the Feel for Interviewing	✓	review			
Basic Techniques	5 Interview Preparation		✓	review	✓	
	6 Conducting a Business Interview		✓	review		
	7 Note-taking		✓	review		
	8 Using the Interview Material		✓	review		
Advanced Techniques	9 Advanced Techniques			✓		
	10 Special Interview Management		✓	✓	✓	
	11 Interviewing in a Business System Life Cycle	✓	✓	✓	✓	✓
	References and Further Reading	✓	✓	✓	✓	✓
	Appendices and Glossary	✓	✓	✓	✓	✓

Chapter

2

A SIMPLE EXAMPLE

Before we look at the details of various interviewing techniques, let us take an example from a hypothetical company and see how an interview might be conducted. We will then look at how the interview might affect the future activities within the company and why the interview was important.

The Interview Situation

Our company, an airline called Atlantis Island Flights, operates flights from the island group Atlantis. Following a number of successful years, the company is considering some business diversification. One project is the development of a hotel on the main island to improve the service offered to passengers travelling with the airline and also to attract the local business community. Jill Graham is the executive responsible for the overall success of this project.

Jill has hired the services of Gordon Beam, a consultant whom Chris Hayley (the Personnel Director) has used very successfully on a previous project. After discussions with the leading local architectural practice, Gordon suggests that Alan Scott, the chief architect, joins him for the first few interviews as a way of getting an early involvement in the project. Alan jumps at the opportunity and volunteers to take notes, as he is less sure of his interviewing technique!

The Scene

Jill Graham is in her office dictating a letter to her secretary Leslie. Gordon Beam and Alan Scott (who has been given the task of developing blueprints for the hotel) arrive fifteen minutes early for an interview with Miss Graham.

She sees them arrive and checks her watch, then waves them into the office as she finishes the letter.

Jill Graham

"... and I therefore expect a refund of at least half of my bill. Yours faithfully etc., etc."

She stands up to greet them:

"That's all for now, thank you, Leslie. Can you make sure that letter is in today's post and could we have some coffee please. Ah, good morning, come in and sit down."

They shake hands and Gordon introduces Alan Scott.

Alan Scott

"Good morning, Miss Graham; that sounds like an interesting way to start the week."

He nods towards the notes that Jill's secretary has taken.

Jill Graham

"Yes, the letter is to the manager of the hotel where I stayed last night – appalling service. It has annoyed me so much that I have demanded a refund."

They sit down: Jill Graham in her executive chair; Alan and Gordon across the desk in the visitors' chairs.

Figure 2-1
The Initial Seating
Arrangement

Gordon Beam

Preparing himself by removing books and papers from his case:

"Sounds pretty serious, what happened?"

Jill Graham

"Oh, amazing incompetence. I was already rather late for my flight because it took so long to check out. The hotel computer system was down and the cashier was having problems working out my bill; he couldn't even add it up until he found a calculator! Then they managed to lose my case full of important papers. The porter had confused it

with someone else's luggage. If I hadn't spotted it, it would have been loaded into another person's taxi."

Gordon Beam	*"That sounds infuriating: perhaps we can do something with our hotel to make sure things like that don't happen."*
Jill Graham	*"I've been thinking about it – we should be able to do something really professional to make sure that people staying with us don't have to worry about co-ordinating luggage, flights, baggage checks, and so on. I wonder whether we couldn't even work together with the airport authorities to have baggage checks and check-in done in the hotel itself."*
Gordon Beam	*"That's interesting – how would you see that working?"*
Jill Graham	*"I'm not sure exactly – I just know that at present when I travel I personally put a lot of time and energy into moving luggage around, having it checked and weighed, waiting to identify and collect it, escorting it to a taxi, and so on. What I would like, ideally, would be to get off the plane, get transport quickly to the hotel, check in and go up to my room to find all my luggage already there. And on the return journey, it would be great if I could have someone locate me when it's getting near departure time and organize transport to the airport for me and my luggage – separately, if necessary. In fact, I shouldn't need to do anything at all until I get off the aircraft at the other end!"*

Alan Scott is taking careful notes as Jill Graham speaks.

Jill Graham	*"No, I take back that last bit. I think that's going a bit too far – I'll be asking someone to eat my meals on the plane next!"*

They all laugh.

Jill Graham	*"Rather more seriously, the security side of it would be tricky."*
Gordon Beam	*"Yes, but the basic idea is very good – focusing on making it easy for the traveller, as we discussed at the initial briefing."*
Jill Graham	*"Yes, I suppose so."*
Gordon Beam	*"Could I just recap briefly on what we are trying to achieve here today?"*
Jill Graham	*"Please do."*
Gordon Beam	*"Alright. I have jotted down a reminder of the process on this sheet of paper."*

He moves his chair around to the side of the desk so that Jill and he can see the paper the right way up. He then quickly outlines the process and where this interview fits into it (see Figure 2-2).

Figure 2-2
The Interview in Context

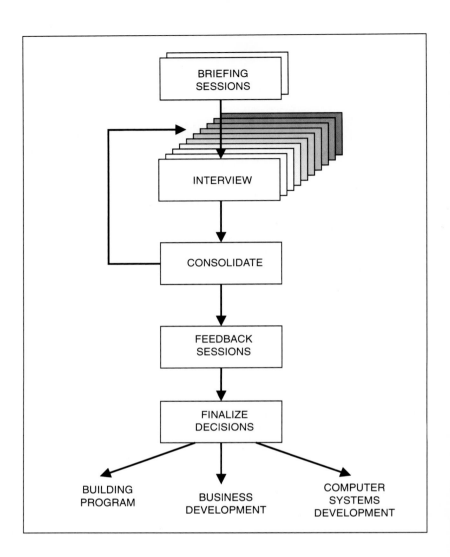

Gordon Beam   *"... so today we are going to explore your overall aims, constraints and initial ideas so that I can prepare a far more accurate brief for the rest of the scheduled interviews. You and I and the rest of the interviewing team will need to do some consolidation, then we will get everyone back together for a feedback session in six weeks' time to check it out. We will use the results from that to derive the design itself."*

Jill Graham   *"That sounds okay to me."*

Gordon Beam   *"We'd also like to record the session, if you don't mind. It helps clarify things if we can't remember what was said. As we said in the briefing session, the tapes will be kept confidential within the team."*

Jill Graham	*"Fine."*

He sets up the tape recorder as the coffee arrives.

Gordon Beam	*"Good. In that case, let's return to your reasons for building this hotel. We were talking about making the hotel easy for travellers to use – what other aims do you have?"*
Jill Graham	*"Well, in line with our policy of serving the local business community, I want to provide conference, meeting and entertainment facilities for local businesses, regardless of whether or not they use the airline. The local business community currently focuses on the tourist trade on the islands but, with the improving communications, we have a growing community of non-tourist businesses and we expect that to continue expanding in the future. At present, there are precious few facilities for these businesses on the island."*
Gordon Beam	*"So the aim is to improve facilities for the non-tourist community on the island?"*
Jill Graham	*"That's right."*
Gordon Beam	*"How will you know if you are succeeding? Or for that matter, failing?"*
Jill Graham	*"What do you mean?"*
Gordon Beam	*"What will determine success or failure towards this goal? How will you know you have 'finished' improving the facilities?"*
Jill Graham	*"H'm – that's difficult – I haven't given much thought to measuring it."*
Gordon Beam	*"Perhaps if we started by examining aspects that you would consider as 'positive' – that is, they help achieve the goal – and things that are 'negative' – in other words, they detract from the goal?"*
Jill Graham	*"Well – we could tell if we were on the right track by the feedback from local businesses – you know, local contacts, the executives we know personally, and so on. There is quite a close, almost a family type of spirit amongst us on the islands, so we tend to find out what is going on in terms of development and future plans ..."*

She sinks back in her chair and her attention begins to wander – she is clearly losing focus on the point and starting to ramble a little! (Is this due to jet lag or Gordon Beam's interviewing technique?)

We can step back from the example briefly and look at what has happened so far. There are three important aspects to this interview that have shaped the event significantly. The first is that Gordon Beam and Alan Scott are well prepared. They have organized the time, room and attended to other logistics so that they arrive in the right place ready to go; a vital component of any interview is to get started well. Speaking of getting started, the second point to notice is the way the interview got under way – Gordon and Alan broke the ice with a short incidental conversation with Jill on a topical subject (in this case her experience with a poorly run hotel) which gently led them into the 'real' interview in a very natural way. Gordon stops briefly after a short while to restate what they hope to achieve during the interview and to start focusing on the main topic of conversation – Jill's project. An easy-going and natural start to an interview helps to set the tone and put the interviewee at ease. Third, and probably most importantly, Gordon is using an open questioning technique – asking questions that do not have simple 'yes/no' answers. The effect of this is that Jill is doing most of the talking (thus supplying information). Gordon maintains continuity by picking up on what Jill says and asking the next related open question. Open questions allow the interviewee to contribute fully during an interview.

We rejoin the interview as Jill has started to ramble and Gordon feels they are not getting much useful information any more ...

Gordon Beam (interrupting politely)	*"Yes, I can see that would be very useful to know. I am particularly interested in something you said earlier – about feedback from the local business community. I wonder whether there is any tangible way of measuring that?"*
Jill Graham	*"I can't think of any way – only subjective assessment."*
Gordon Beam	*"Other companies I have visited sometimes set themselves objectives, like getting local figures to publicly endorse a product or service as a way of measuring this kind of subjective feeling."*
Jill Graham	*"Oh I see! So you mean something like getting well-known local businessmen to market the hotel for us? Yes, that's a good idea – I like it. This is off the top of my head now, but it would be really good to aim for good reviews about the hotel facilities in the local trade journal. People take a lot more notice when the writer is independent, so maybe we should try and get some local business users to consider writing about events they have held at the hotel. You know, I can't help thinking that this is all well and good, but what makes the difference is whether or not people actually use the facilities, so in absolute terms we are going to have to get a certain level of use of the facilities in order to make enough money to stay viable."*
Gordon Beam	*"What level of business would you need?"*
Jill Graham	*"Well, for a start, we would like to get the lion's share of the local conference business. We estimate there are three major events plus ten minor events per week. Major events would last, say, three days on*

average with over two hundred people in attendance; and minor ones about a day or a day and a half with between five and thirty people attending."

Gordon Beam   *"And the lion's share of that would be?"*

Jill Graham   *"Two out of three major events and seven out of ten minor events. And the number of these events is expected to grow at about twenty to forty per cent per year over the next couple of years."*

Gordon Beam   *"So the volume and mix of business that you will be catering for will be changing over time?"*

Jill Graham   *"That's right."*

Gordon Beam   *"What effect will these changes have on the hotel?"*

Jill Graham   *"That's a good question. It means that, initially, we will want to cater for more small parties with short stopovers but, as larger companies become established here, I can see a need for more people staying for longer periods, so one very direct effect will be the need for facilities for larger conferences as time goes on."*

Gordon Beam   *"Yes, I think I understand – you are saying that, currently, we need to cater for smaller groups but, over time, there will be larger groups with longer, more ambitious conferences."*

Jill Graham   *"Yes."*

Gordon Beam	*"How do you think we should adapt to this change?"*
Jill Graham	*"Well, I am very keen to ensure that we blend in with the community appropriately – nothing ostentatious initially – but we are going to need to extend the facilities as time goes by; we probably need to consider convertible accommodation."*
Gordon Beam	*"What do you mean by 'convertible' accommodation?"*
Jill Graham	*"Oh, perhaps a ballroom with partitions that could be brought across to make two separate, small conference halls, for example."*
Gordon Beam	*"Ah – I see – facilities that can have multiple uses."*
Jill Graham	*"That's the sort of thing – I wondered whether it would be possible to construct a building designed to be extended in phases: you know, add further floors or additional wings."*
Alan Scott	*"Or underground levels?"*
Jill Graham	*"Oh! That's a good idea! That would be the sort of thing I would like to do if we could – be unobtrusive, fit into the landscape – we need to be conscious of the impact on the environment. I imagine that has all sorts of implications for the design and choice of building materials these days, as well as the actual siting of the development."*
Gordon Beam	*"It certainly does: and there are new ideas and regulations coming forward all the time. That's something we will have to consider more and more.*
	I'd just like to go over what we have identified so far. One of the aims is to make it easy for the traveller to use the facilities of the hotel as part of a journey with the airline. And another is to cater for a growing local business community. And you have already set some specific objectives for the second aim: to have two out of every three major events and seven out of every ten minor events held at the hotel. You also want the hotel design to be flexible enough to allow you to convert it for different events and allow the building work to be done in phases. So far we have one constraint – the hotel must meet some environmental standards. I would like to explore that in more detail if we have time, but first, are there any other specific aims you have set for the hotel?"

Gordon and Jill continue for a further half hour exploring more fully all Jill's aspirations, goals and constraints on the hotel project. They are interrupted by the arrival of a much needed cup of coffee.

Jill Graham	*"Ah, coffee! Good, I could use this – I didn't think this was going to be such hard work!"*

Gordon Beam	*"Yes, I know how hard it can be trying to cover such a lot of ground, but we like to get as much as possible out in the open right at the beginning of the process to avoid the disappointment of not meeting expectations later."*
Jill Graham	*"I understand. Please don't apologize; it is quite good fun and it's helping me get my thoughts in order as well."*
Gordon Beam	*"Well, in that case, I would like to go into a bit more detail on a few things. Earlier, we spoke about a possible check-in service and ballroom and conference facilities. What other facilities do you see the hotel offering?"*
Jill Graham	*"Well, clearly, there would be the usual accommodation, restaurant and bar: perhaps two restaurants – to cater for the traveller in a hurry on the one hand and the businessman entertaining a client on the other. A pool, a fitness centre and a games-room could be useful. We aren't aiming at the tourist market, but people attending conferences often like to use these facilities too – for a bit of exercise before the start of the working day or to unwind at the end of the day. But, most importantly, I think we should be able to offer services that link up with the airline and the airport."*
Gordon Beam	*"I see. What sort of thing do you have in mind?"*

The interview progresses for a further two hours, extended at Jill Graham's request, exploring ideas for the operation of the hotel.

Gordon Beam	*"... OK. If I were to sum up my understanding of what you are after, it is a hotel to take advantage of a business opportunity on the island, closely linked to the traveller using the island airport, and Atlantis Island Flights in particular, with an initially small, but growing, provision for local business activities. Regarding style, we are looking for something that is perceived as high quality, without being ostentatious, and fitting in with the local environment; and all closely linked to the activities of the airport for the traveller, which we should follow up with Ed Singer and his people."*
Jill Graham	*"Yes, that's a reasonable summary."*
Gordon Beam	*"Good. Now, before we finish, are there any other points you think we ought to have covered which we have missed?"*
Jill Graham	*"No, I don't think so. But, I do want to emphasize what I said about being able to build in phases, so that we have a choice of when we commit ourselves to the growth, in case our expectations turn out to be over-optimistic – and, also, when the right time comes, we can expand without undue pressure on existing facilities."*

Gordon Beam	*"I understand. We need to plan for catering, laundry and other facilities to expand in order to cope with the throughput as it grows, but without committing to the building of large kitchens, and so on, initially."*
Jill Graham	*"That's the sort of thing – yes."*
Gordon Beam	*"Alright – anything else?"*
Jill Graham	*"No, I don't think so."*
Gordon Beam	*"There is just one thing I thought you might have mentioned that we didn't cover, and that is the question of local amenities – theatres, shops, sporting facilities, and so on. What would the relationship be with these?"*
Jill Graham	*"Well – a kind of Jekyll and Hyde, I suspect. We would do well to work closely with these businesses: not only will it make the hotel more attractive if we can offer good terms with local sporting facilities, and so on, but we ought to provide them with a marvellous supply of customers. On the other hand, with some of them we will be in direct competition; the restaurants, for example. But I would like to keep a friendly local community spirit about the whole thing – after all, some of these small businesses may become our biggest sources of revenue in the future."*
Gordon Beam	*"Well, thank you for giving us so much of your time this morning, Jill. We will work on these ideas and directions, plus any others we pick up over the next week or so, and we will try to devise a consolidated set of objectives and facilities for the feedback meeting in six weeks' time. Alan will sketch a few initial ideas to see how you all react to them, so we are sure that we're on the right track."*
Jill Graham	*"I will look forward to that."*

The actual interview is now over, but for Alan Scott and Gordon Beam their work on what they have just learned is not finished. They will need to work together to review the interview as soon as possible while it is still fresh in their minds. Alan, as note-taker, must now consolidate his notes. During the interview Gordon also made some notes, and it will be interesting in their follow-up discussion to see if they picked up the same messages from the interviewee.

How the Interview May Affect the Project

The way an interview is conducted and the interaction that results can affect the progress of a project as much as the information gathered during the interview. As a result of this example interview, a number of aspects of the Atlantis project change.

Trust and Commitment in the Project Team

Jill feels comfortable that Gordon is capable of controlling an interview, so she can rely on him to let everyone have a say and express their own ideas. As a result, she can relax her own involvement just a little, giving her more time to worry about the strategic implications of the hotel and how to make the project a success.

Information

Gordon Beam uses the information gained to start constructing structured models of what is required and uses these as a framework to prepare for future interviews. This means that the interviews are well structured and controlled (kept relevant and 'to the point'), leaving each person feeling that he or she has contributed fully. Many of the contributions are in conflict with each other, but Gordon Beam runs a workshop to make the tough decisions in a way that the group can all live with.

Early Involvement

Alan Scott is grateful for being involved early; as an architect, he said he would not have believed such short timescales were achievable with so many influential people involved. He accredits some of his own ability to produce accurate outlines and mock-ups to a thorough understanding of what each person thinks is important.

Commitment from the Management

With such a clear opportunity to express their own personal views and a chance to resolve issues in a controlled workshop, the management team at Atlantis Island Flights have all said how committed they feel to the project, born out of a common understanding of what is needed. Much of this feeling of commitment is attributed to a good start with interviews, where they are encouraged to speak their minds frankly and fully.

Summary

We have introduced a simple example of an interview, with the purpose of gathering information. Gordon Beam and Alan Scott have acquired some important information from Jill Graham; and not just facts – they have also established an idea of how Jill **feels** about the project and what she considers to be of prime importance.

Chapter

3   BASIC INTERVIEWING

Introduction

The short example in Chapter 2 illustrates the application of some basic interviewing techniques. In this chapter we will highlight these techniques and describe them in more detail.

You may have thought that this example interview was like a fairly easygoing conversation, albeit a conversation with a purpose rather than mere social discourse, and that is how an interview should be – conducted with ease and a lack of visible effort. The interviewer using these techniques should do so in an unobtrusive and natural manner, so that both interviewer and interviewee are relaxed and making good use of the time given to the interview.

An interview, however, actually entails far more than just the time spent in the discussion itself. We like to think of the process in three phases:

- Planning
- Conducting the interview and
- Consolidation.

These will be covered briefly in overview in this chapter, using illustrations from the example in Chapter 2.

Topics covered in this chapter include knowing your objectives, preparation, open and closed questions, rapport, control and consolidating and using information. The entire interviewing process is examined in more detail in Chapters 5 to 8.

The People and their Roles

In the most basic interview situation two people will meet for a discussion, one person being the interviewer and one the interviewee. The interviewer is usually a person with good listening skills who can keep a conversation going (sometimes called 'active listening') and the interviewee is the person who (hopefully) has some information of use to the interviewer. We like to keep interviews to a single interviewee if possible (people are generally more forthcoming when not in the company of their peers or management). However, interviewing two, three or more people together can yield useful information. For many interviews, especially a short meeting with a clear aim, having a single interviewee and interviewer will work well. But imagine you have a wide-ranging discussion that lasts two, three or even more hours. How are you going to remember all the important points that the interview has revealed? You will need notes. You could tape record the discussion – and then spend as long again trying to pick out the salient points. Or you could take notes yourself during the interview – with the risk that you may be so busy trying to get things written down that it distracts you from listening or distracts your interviewee from talking. The ideal solution is to have a note-taker, so the interviewer is free to concentrate on the business of interviewing.

What sort of person should take these notes? If you want a verbatim copy of the interview a good shorthand writer is the answer (or somebody that can write longhand very quickly!). If you want a compact set of notes where key ideas, constraints, actions, and so on, have been identified, choose a good analyst. In fact, when assigning people to the roles of interviewer and note-taker, you should give the role of note-taker to a good analyst. Generally the note-taker keeps a fairly low profile during the interview; but someone may, for example, wish to refer back to a point raised earlier in the interview and a skilled note-taker can use this as an opportunity to contribute to the direction of the interview rather than mere feedback of information. There is no reason why the interviewer and note-taker should not swap roles part-way through the interview. We cover roles and techniques in much greater depth in the chapters on Interview Preparation, Conducting a Business Interview and Note-taking.

Planning

Knowing your Objectives

An interview has been described as a *"conversation with a purpose"* (Gratus, 1988). By defining the purpose of the interview you have stated your main objective – knowing what you are trying to achieve is an essential part of the whole process.

An objective or **aim** of an interview is some outcome that you are trying to achieve by conducting the interview. You should be able to state: *"As a result of this interview, we will have succeeded if ..."* followed by a list of the outcomes you are seeking. Imagine you are a family doctor and a patient has arrived for a consultation. You are going to have a conversation with the patient and the purpose is to establish the most likely cause of the symptoms the patient describes. Some aims and objectives you may set yourself are:

- to gain and retain the patient's confidence
- to establish a complete list of symptoms
- to find out if the patient has any preconceived ideas of the causes
- to take less than ten minutes.

Try setting objectives for some other scenarios: as a parent you are going to meet the head teacher of the school you are thinking of sending your daughter to. Or, as a builder you are going to discuss a large and lucrative contract with a prospective client. It can also be revealing to consider what the interviewee may hope to get from an interview. You will probably find some general objectives that could apply to almost any interview, and others that are specific to a particular interview. Here are some suggestions that can apply to almost any interview:

- make the most of the interviewee's time
- add value for the interviewee
- get the information you need
- enjoy it.

In our example in the previous chapter, Gordon Beam set himself two aims for his interview with Jill Graham:

- to establish her aspirations for the new hotel (i.e. the aims for the **project** itself) and

- to illustrate his own ability to understand what she needs from the project, thereby increasing her trust in him as an individual.

Ask yourself what kind of information you need to obtain or give during an interview. Clear-cut objectives will help you to guide the conversation and give you reference points during the interview, enabling you to ask the question: *"Is this helping to achieve the objectives I set for the interview?"* If you are not making progress towards your objectives, you will probably need to use some of the control techniques described later. Consciously stating the objectives for an interview also helps to determine whether or not a key area of interest has been adequately covered.

Different kinds of interviews have different aims. Consider the talk show – the aim is to entertain; or the news broadcast from the scene of a crime – the aim is to uncover facts and feelings about the event; whereas the aim of a journalist interviewing a politician is usually to trap the politician into telling the truth or, failing that, to provoke him or her into saying something controversial! A common type of interview in a business context is questioning applicants for a job or position. The **aim** in such an interview is to discover which interviewee is the most appropriate for the job.

In this book we will concentrate on interviews that are used to obtain information from people running a business organization, with a view to using that information to change the business in some way or to develop relevant business support systems. (Many of the techniques discussed are also applicable to other types of interview.) The main purpose of such interviews is usually to discover or check our understanding of key aspects of the business: what drives it (the mission and objectives for an organization), those factors critical to the success (or failure) of a business, the current strengths and weaknesses of the organization, what the business does (or needs to do), and what information is necessary in order to do it effectively. A second, and very important, aspect of this kind of interview is that of uncovering (and possibly affecting) the politics, power struggles and other 'people-related' issues in an organization.

Objectives give us a reference point for guiding the conversation. Consider them as you would a compass – acting as a directional guide.

Preparation

An old maxim with some relevance here is: *"time spent in reconnaissance is never wasted"*. For a two-hour interview, it would not be unusual for a skilled interviewer and note-taker to spend two hours or more each in preparation beforehand. Typically, this preparation would include:

- background reading
- assembling an interviewee profile
- drawing up checklists
- contingency planning
- organizing rooms, schedules, and so on.

Although this may sound like a long time it is frequently inadequate, so plan ahead and make sure you allow yourself enough preparation time.

Background Research

Background research, or 'doing your homework', involves finding out as much relevant information as possible about the situation. Your objectives will help to decide what is, and is not, relevant. Material can be found from various sources, such as:

- external sources; for example, industry analysts' or stockbrokers' reports
- marketing literature (brochures etc.)
- observation (go and watch the company in action)
- advertisements
- the company's annual reports
- an employee handbook
- policy and procedures manuals
- published plans.

In one study for a rental business, we went out and rented some equipment from one of its shops: we became customers in order to gain some first-hand experience of dealing with the organization.

Look for information about the business, such as how much profit it made last year, how its success is measured, and so on, to get a feeling for the scale of its activities. Read reports of special interest to the interviewee. These reports may contain insights into the interviewee as a person or information of particular relevance. In turn, this helps to form an understanding of what is familiar and important to the interviewee, so that you will be better prepared during the interview. You can gain credibility as someone who knows the background situation, an especially important quality when interviewing senior managers who cannot afford to waste time because the interviewer is ignorant of some very basic background information. Eliminating basic questions, or possibly confirming basic information, early in the interview allows you more time to explore details. This results in more topics being covered in the time available, thus making good use of the interviewee's time.

If you work for the company yourself you may feel you already know all you need to about the organization. In fact, this can be a disadvantage because it can lead to you, the interviewer, making false assumptions. Pretend you are an external consultant who is completely unfamiliar with the company, so that you are looking at it with a fresh pair of eyes.

In our example, Gordon Beam did his homework before the interview. He had already established how many passengers travelled to and from the island via the airport and the overall business aims and aspirations of

Atlantis Island Flights from the recent annual report and, with Alan, had spoken to an old friend at the local government planning office about the possibility of a new hotel and how that would be viewed by the planning authority.

Interviewee Profile

It is important to get to know a little about your interviewee prior to the interview. This information helps you plan appropriate questions and warns you about sensitive areas. For instance, the interviewee may only have held her present position for a few weeks, which would limit how much you could expect to learn about her current situation and future plans! In addition to a brief career history, it is useful to know some other details about the people you are going to interview:

- What are their pet subjects, likes, dislikes?
- How do their staff and managers describe them?
- What are their special interests, hobbies?

Background information gives you a basis for establishing rapport with an interviewee and provides you with good 'ice-breakers' at the beginning of the interview. These are spontaneous, informal comments related to the person's interests: *"How did your golf tournament go last weekend? I see you have a model of the latest engine you make – can you show me the new features? How is your Bernese Mountain dog?"*

Sometimes the occasion of the interview may itself provide the opening, as in our example in Chapter 2:

Alan Scott	*"Good morning, Miss Graham; that sounds like an interesting way to start the week."* He nods towards the notes that Jill's secretary has taken.
Jill Graham	*"Yes, the letter is to the manager of the hotel where I stayed last night – appalling service. It has annoyed me so much that I have demanded a refund."*

There is more to preparation, however, than the information side. With the objectives defined and some background information gathered, we are now ready to begin preparing checklists and questions.

Checklists

A checklist is a list of words or phrases that represent topics you would expect the interviewee to talk about. It can also jog your memory if you are looking for the next question. At the end of an interview this list can be used as a 'sweep up' to check that everything has been covered. For example, in the interview in Chapter 2, Gordon Beam would have picked up the following item from his checklist:

> *"There is just one thing I thought you might have mentioned that we didn't cover, and that is the question of local amenities – theatres, shops, sporting facilities, and so on. What would our relationship be with these?"*

During the interview, if you note which areas have been covered by crossing them off your checklist, you will be able to see at a glance which areas still require questions. In an unstructured interview, one without a set list of actual questions, a checklist provides a framework for the discussion to make sure that everything is covered. In this way, the natural flow of the conversation is maintained, with the checklist serving as a cross-check rather than as a predetermined sequence of questions.

For business interviews, we often suggest two checklists: one general, one topical. The general list covers strategic or high-level business topics, such as the market, competitors, critical success factors in the industry, and so on. These topics form the basis for questions that will be put to each interviewee when a number of interviews are being conducted. By asking similar questions of a number of well-chosen people, who represent the whole organization, a good picture of areas of consensus and differences can be obtained, which helps to establish a complete picture. The second checklist is more specific to the area of responsibility or specialization of the interviewee. For example, a personnel director can provide answers in the detailed area of human resources and the topical checklist will identify key points to discuss in that functional area. The double checklist used by Gordon Beam is shown below.

Figure 3-1
Checklist for Interview with Jill Graham

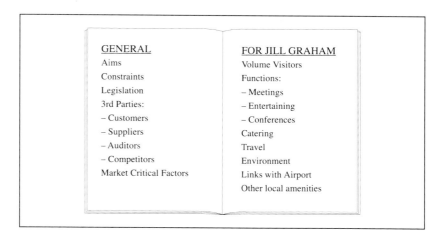

You may want to modify the list during the interview, as other ideas arise from the discussion. Write them down to remind you, should you want to explore them further later on in the interview. You can even have opening and closing questions written on your checklist beforehand, turning it into an interview template, but bear in mind that the interview itself may be a fresh source of these.

Logistics

Diary For May

week 1 . . . .
. . . .
week 2 . . . .
. . . .
week 3 . . . .
. . . .
week 4 . . . .
. . . .

Where? When? What will it be about? For how long? What should I do beforehand? Questions like these will occur to the interviewee when you get in touch to arrange an interview. The ideal situation is a comfortable, quiet location with no interruptions and plenty of time, but this can be hard to arrange, especially with busy senior managers. We have interviewed people on trains, in taxis, even walking around a factory. Sometimes you have to take whatever you can get. But more often than not there is some choice of location and you can arrange for it to meet the needs of an interview.

Appendix D provides a full checklist of things you might like to consider, but a short list would include:

- a comfortable room
- refreshments organized
- interruptions minimized (e.g. a secretary asked to hold all telephone calls)
- appointments for the interview made (then confirmed and reconfirmed right up to the day of the interview).

For a general, unstructured interview, it is often better to ask the interviewee **not** to prepare for it in advance. This should allow you to judge the person's true feelings and emotional commitment to a subject, which could be hidden by a prepared script. At one interview recently, the interviewee used up the **entire** time allotted to the interview to take us through a prepared presentation on 35mm slides in a darkened room! Needless to say, this did not really count as an interview at all.

Contingency Planning

Finally, remember to do some contingency planning – prepare yourself for things that could go wrong. What will you do if the room you booked is not available? Your note-taker does not turn up? The interviewee has to rush out to an emergency meeting? Or is hostile? Or silent? Contingency planning can reduce the risk of a bad interview should there be a problem. Imagine an interviewee who is silent, hostile or simply does not like you – this could lead to an uncomfortable and unproductive interview.

You may ask if there is anything you can **plan** in case the subject is hostile. Clearly, a detailed plan of what to do is not possible. The action you take depends on the circumstances, but it is helpful to imagine what you **could** do so that you are at least partially prepared. You could perhaps swap roles between note-taker and interviewer or even directly ask the interviewee why he or she is being unco-operative. These situations are not easy to handle, although there are a few more suggestions in

Chapter 6. All we would suggest at this stage is that you think through all the things you can imagine going wrong and give yourself the benefit of the experience, even if it is only imaginary.

During the interview, basic techniques for interviewing include asking questions, establishing rapport, and gaining and maintaining control of the situation. These fundamentals are used by every interviewer. To get you in the right frame of mind for an information-collecting business interview, imagine you are going to take this person's job tomorrow and you have only the one interview to get enough information to survive.

We always like to plan for two or three extra interviews. An interviewee may recommend talking to someone you did not previously know about, an expert in a particular field, for example. These additional interviews may not be needed and the arrangements can be cancelled in that event.

Figure 3-2
Summary of Planning and Preparing for an Interview

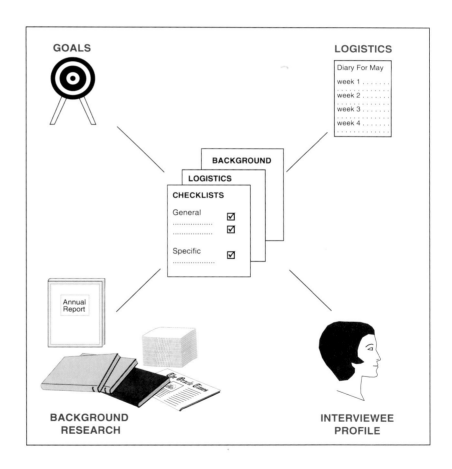

Conducting the Interview

Open Questions

If you observe and listen to a **good** interviewer, perhaps a well-known talk show host, you will find he or she begins sessions with some general questions to get the interviewee talking freely. Questions such as *"Have you ever been to Berlin? Have you met Mr Johnson yet? How often do you go to the cinema? Is that a new pair of shoes?"* obviously invite factual answers. They are not designed to open up a discussion.

An open question is a question that cannot be answered with a one-word or very short reply. It invites a free-ranging reply, which then forms the basis for related follow-up questions. The main point of using open questions is to avoid influencing or slanting the interview with ideas and preconceptions from the interviewer. A really open question gives the interviewee a completely free choice of how to answer. Illustrations of open questions from the example in the last chapter include:

> *"How will you know if you are succeeding? Or for that matter, failing?"*
> *"What will determine success or failure towards this goal?"*
> *"What level of business would you need?"*
> *"What effect will these changes have on the hotel?"*

Like these examples, open questions can indeed begin with interrogative words like what and how and why, although questions framed like this often invite short factual answers: *"What is your latest book called? How will I recognize him? When will the new office be ready?"* Sometimes the actual words used in an open question are not strictly a question at all, more of an invitation to talk about something: *"Tell me about the ballet you are directing. Tell me about the computer system you use at present."*

Another technique that promotes open-ended replies is for the interviewer to make a statement that can be elaborated on by the person being interviewed. Again, this is not strictly speaking a question, but it serves the same purpose as an open question if it elicits a response that promotes a free discussion. One of the first statements in the interview of Chapter 2 illustrates a good, informal opener:

> *"Good morning, Miss Graham; that sounds like an interesting way to start the week."*

Gordon Beam and Alan Scott have raised a subject of immediate concern to the interviewee, so this almost casual opening comment evokes an interesting response:

> *"Yes, the letter is to the manager of the hotel where I stayed last night – appalling service. It has annoyed me so much that I have demanded a refund."*

which in turn provides an opportunity to ask a follow-on question:

> *"Sounds pretty serious, what happened?"*

Although this short question appears to be asking for a factual answer, the lengthy reply from Jill Graham raises a number of interesting points about hotel bills and checking out and getting you and your luggage to the airport in time. In lieu of a question, Gordon Beam makes another statement:

> *"That sounds infuriating: perhaps we can do something with our hotel to make sure things like that don't happen."*

which stimulates all sorts of ideas from the interviewee.

Let us look again at the sequence – there is an informal greeting and introductory statement that encourages the interviewee to talk about an incident that is uppermost in her mind. This creates a framework for an open-ended interchange by establishing rapport and showing an understanding and interest in the interviewee. It is only after this initial informal interchange, which goes on for some time, that the purpose of the interview is formally introduced by the interviewer showing Jill Graham a diagram. He also moves his chair so that he is sitting next to her, rather than in the more formal and perhaps confrontational position opposite. At this point, a focused interview begins. These techniques have enabled the interviewer to set the tone within the first few minutes and interviewer and interviewee feel comfortable with one another.

As the interview progresses, other open questions are used to elicit specific information that Gordon Beam needs:

> *"Good. In that case, let's return to your reasons for building this hotel. We were talking about making the hotel easy for travellers to use – what other aims do you have?"*

He wants to know the overall aims of the project. To get this information accurately he must ensure that the interviewee knows exactly what he means by an aim, so he frames a previous statement (making the hotel easy for travellers to use) as an aim to give her a clear example and then asks the question. Citing an example and asking for other examples to obtain more detail is another useful line of questioning:

> *"... I would like to go into a bit more detail on a few things ... we spoke about a possible check-in service ... What other facilities do you see the hotel offering?"*

Other probing questions are asked in order to define aspects of the project more clearly, for example:

> *"Perhaps if we started by examining aspects that you would consider as 'positive' – that is, they help achieve the goal – and things that are 'negative' – in other words, they detract from the goal?"*

Suggestions can also become open-ended questions and often have the bonus of providing a sense of added value to the interviewee's situation. In our example, Gordon Beam and Jill Graham start considering how the hotel will cater for changes in the volume and mix of its business and Jill Graham suggests the idea of 'convertible' accommodation. A subsequent suggestion for this by the architect Alan Scott:

> *"Or underground levels?"*

is well received (*"Oh! That's a good idea!"*) and provides a useful link into the important issue of environmental standards.

So far in our discussion we have focused mainly on questions that the interviewer already had in mind. It is possible, however, to overlook significant areas and a good question to ask towards the end of an interview, while still leaving sufficient time for exploration, is: *"Are there any topics you planned to discuss today that we have not covered?"* Note how Gordon Beam provides sufficient time to ask:

> *"Good. Now, before we finish, are there any other points you think we ought to have covered which we have missed?"*

In this case, no new point is raised but it presents the interviewee with the chance to re-emphasize a particular point. Sometimes major new topics are introduced at this time. The interviewee may well have planned to discuss things that have not yet been covered. This is an opportunity for the interviewee to raise these matters and complete the interview feeling satisfied that everything he or she thinks is important has been covered.

There are many types of open questions, or statements that can act as such. Here are a few examples from Chapter 2:

- informal introductory statements – *"Good morning. That sounds ..."*
- statements to elicit open replies – *"That sound infuriating: perhaps we can do something ..."*

- framing an example to draw out similar information – *"... making the hotel easy for travellers to use – what other aims do you have?"*

- suggestions to test ideas and initiate others – *"Or underground levels?"*

- probing for details with examples – *"... check-in service . . . What other facilities . . .?"*

- verifying general coverage of topics in the interview – *"Now, before we finish ... is there anything else? ..."*

- checklist questions – look again at the checklist in Figure 3-1 to see how many of these open questions relate to this list.

An intense and productive period of open-ended questioning can be exhausting, yet you hesitate to break the flow of creative discussion. Should you feel your interviewee is beginning to flag, it can be helpful to intersperse the free-ranging discussion with some less demanding but still relevant questions. When Gordon Beam asks how much the lion's share of the conference business would be, Jill Graham is able to give him quite exact figures readily.

Closed Questions

```
 ?  ?
? ?  ?
 ?  ?
```

A closed question is a question that can be answered with a simple yes or no or a short factual answer. For instance:

"How many aircraft use the airport each day?"
"Do you think the passenger check-in could be done in the hotel?"
"What is your telephone number?"

They are used where you need to get specific facts, such as the planned opening date for the hotel on Atlantis or the number of seats on a given aeroplane. Another use is to check the interviewer's understanding. Imagine consulting your doctor about a pain in your abdomen, and the doctor prods you and asks: *"Is this where it hurts?"* Answers will tend to be short (yes, no, ouch, etc.).

Every so often during an interview you may want to recap, or summarize what you have just been discussing, inviting the person being interviewed to say whether or not you have understood correctly. This is perhaps a bit like the take-away pizza place repeating your order: *"So that's a small pepperoni, a medium cheese and tomato with extra anchovies, a portion of garlic bread and two salads?"* The 'summary inviting confirmation' is a useful technique, but it should be used with care. In our example interview, Jill Graham and Gordon Beam have been discussing local business use of the proposed hotel in some depth:

Jill Graham	*"... we would like to get the lion's share of the local conference business ... Two out of three major events and seven out of ten minor events. And the number of these events is expected to grow at about twenty to forty per cent per year over the next couple of years."*
	The consultant asks a question that invites an answer of yes:
Gordon Beam	*"So the volume and mix of business that you will be catering for will be changing over time?"*

The interviewee agrees (*"That's right"*), but a more careful examination of what she has actually said shows that her interviewer has fallen into the common trap of getting agreement by the way the question is phrased. Yes the volume of business is expected to change, but no mention was made of a change of mix, although it would not be an unreasonable assumption. And how much change is likely? One of them may envisage a modest increase in volume with a major change in the mix of business, while the other may envisage a massive increase in overall trade but much the same mix. Loosely worded questions can lead to superficial or casual agreement, not agreement based on a thorough exploration of the issues. The cause of the problem here is that the question is too general and leaves much to individual interpretation, allowing two people to apparently agree on a statement, while retaining different interpretations of its meaning. Whenever you seek clarification using closed questions, make those questions as definitive and unambiguous as possible.

Consider the effect of rephrasing Gordon Beam's question:

"Will the volume of business change over time and also, will the mix of business that you will be catering for change as well?"

It is no longer a summarizing question that almost begs affirmation; and it now has two parts, each of which can be answered yes or no. To clarify the possible changes he will also need to ask for figures for both aspects.

The danger with too many closed questions in close sequence is that they may arrest the flow of the conversation. In fact, what develops may be less like a conversation and more like filling in a survey form. Awkward silences can develop. Judicious mixing of questions is a technique that skilled interviewers use, almost unconsciously. But they do more than just ask the right questions: they also judge the answers. The words may be saying *"Yes, I agree with you"*, but the eyes may belie it. An interviewee may give the answers he thinks you want to hear, or he ought to give, rather than what he genuinely believes himself. The skilled interviewer 'reads the signs', not only listening to the verbal content of these answers, but noticing the non-verbal communications. Of course, your interviewee may start to look uncomfortable because she is developing a muscle cramp in one of her legs, is thirsty, is starting to lose concentration because it is hard work or has just realized she forgot to do something in the office before the interview. (Remember how Gordon Beam turned up fifteen minutes early? Jill Graham finished dictating that letter before starting the interview.) During a long interview, a short break for friendly chatting, say when coffee comes in, and the occasional digression from the main business of the interview can be useful breathers.

The One Minute Interviewing Guide

Think of your interview as a meal with a bowl of spaghetti as the main course. The objective of interviewing someone is to get all of the relevant information that you need out of that person's head in a very short period of time. Imagine sitting down to eat the bowl of spaghetti. One way to clear the bowl would be to start eating one of the strands of spaghetti by pulling and sucking, gradually pulling it out. This is analogous to asking an open question and during the process of answering it you start to ask supplementary questions that pull out more and more information. Over time most of the bowl will be cleared, assuming you have a good set of open questions and the interviewee is forthcoming.

However, as with the bowl of spaghetti, where there are quite a lot of strands left at the bottom of the bowl, there will be important information that you still need to get out. This is where checklist questions come in. An open question in a personnel environment may be: *"Tell me how you run your personnel business?"* Your checklist will contain words like legislation, company policy, retention and global pay rises, which could be converted into open questions to clear the bowl: *"What will be the impact of new legislation?"*, *"Tell me about retention of staff"*.

To continue with our analogy, the hors d'oeuvres at the start of the meal are akin to the initial discussion questions to break the ice and settle the interviewee into the role. Dessert and coffee to complete the meal are like the closing questions, to make sure that you have not missed anything. And during the meal you have the occasional respite from the hard work of eating by sipping a glass of wine – this is like the type of questions used to pick up factual information and give the interviewee time to recover from some of the tough questions you have been asking. There is, of course, no reason why you should not conduct an interview of this nature while having such a meal. However, on such occasions you may have to buy the tablecloth if you write your notes on it!

Listening Skills

Framing the right questions is only half of the task: the interviewer and note-taker must both be good and active listeners. The note-taker in particular must record what is actually said, not what he or she thinks is said. Skills associated with good listening are the ability to:

- empathize – be able to understand the other person's point of view

- listen 'behind' the words – are there any hidden meanings?

- be patient – allow the interviewee to complete the answers, even when he or she is struggling with words

- listen objectively – leave your own prejudices and preconceptions behind: do not impose your own view. Probe to determine the other person's position

- remain quiet – let the interviewee talk

- allow silence – give the interviewee sufficient time to think.

Most of us can talk readily enough with a little encouragement (some of us need no encouragement to expound our own views!). But few of us are good listeners. We 'hear' the words but are not actually listening. How often have you been involved in a discussion where everyone is so busy 'talking at' one another that when others are speaking you can hardly wait for them to stop so that you can continue expressing your own opinions or giving your ideas? This is not so much a discussion (you are not actually listening to each other) as several interrupted monologues. Often what we 'hear' others say is what we want or expect them to say, not what they actually say – a sort of subjective listening, because what is heard is the product of our own preconceptions. A good example of this type of discussion would be a political debate.

Rapport
('Bedside Manner')

We often refer to establishing a rapport with someone. But how do we do that? By rapport we mean something akin to empathy, an ability to relate to and communicate readily with another person. Sometimes when you meet a person for the first time you get on so well that you feel as if you have known each other for years. You warm to each other: a case of instant rapport. More often it takes a little longer to establish a rapport. A seemingly trivial comment can help build the feeling – perhaps about a shared acquaintance, or home town, or about work done for a previous company or some common interest. We all know that good feeling we experience when we discover that someone we are talking to shares similar likes and dislikes – we feel rapport. This is the feeling you want to create in an interview situation. Often some common background can be found in the interviewee profile or from on-the-spot observations of the office surroundings. For instance:

"I see you have a memento from that big contract the company won in '86 on your desk here. I remember that day – it was the day I joined the company ..."

Breaking the Ice

When you arrive (**promptly**, of course), do not make the error of plunging into the main business too quickly. Give yourself a chance to develop rapport and establish a good tone for the interview. This is important because it enables you to open up communications and encourage a comfortable, relaxed atmosphere within the first few minutes of the interview, so that lots of information can be exchanged rapidly and candidly. Promptness can be an important first step, followed by a period of 'getting to know one another'. Rushing into the main business too quickly can make the situation artificial.

Just before the interview, Alan Scott made an on-the-spot observation about the importance of a letter that Jill Graham was dictating. Without being intrusive, he starts the interview on a subject that is of great immediate interest to the interviewee:

"Good morning. That sounds like an interesting way to start the week."

This opening line quickly established rapport and led in a natural way to other questions. Good doctors are skilled at building rapport, only it is usually known as bedside manner in that profession. No doubt you have your own way of breaking the ice. The important point to remember is that it must sound and feel natural and spontaneous. Otherwise, a rehearsed line will sound awkward.

Promptness

This topic merits some further examination: it is a case of a good thing, but you can also have too much of a good thing. At the beginning of the interview, Gordon Beam and Alan Scott arrive early. This gives them time to observe the office environment of the interviewee. Avoid turning up too early, though, as that may put the other person under pressure. Imagine you are due to be interviewed at eleven in the morning. You may have some specific task you want to complete beforehand, but you notice the interviewing team has turned up at ten o'clock (there were no hold ups on the trip in this morning!). If you keep them waiting till the appointed hour you may feel you are being rude. If you start early you may keep worrying that you did not complete that vital task so you will be tense and unable to give them your full attention. Rapport will be in short supply.

Seating

Another factor contributing to rapport is the seating arrangement. Your aim is to place the interviewer and interviewee in an equal position for the duration of the interview – not on opposing sides, which may appear to be the case if you are facing each other across a desk. Ask to sit in chairs side by side if that arrangement is possible in the room, but angle towards each other to allow eye contact, or move your chair to the side of the desk rather than in an opposing stance. You do not want the interviewee (or interviewer) to be dominant. Your aim is to place both of you in a more equal and informal situation for the duration of the interview. The note-taker does not need to have direct eye contact, and a position slightly sideways on will allow the note-taker to observe the facial expressions and body language of the interviewee from a different aspect.

Figure 3-3
Possible Seating
Arrangements for
the Interview

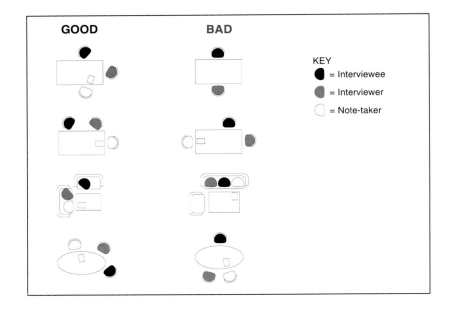

It may be that an ideal arrangement is not possible (if the interviewee has pre-arranged the seating, for instance), in which case you may need to try one or more of the control techniques discussed in Chapter 6. In the example in Chapter 2, Gordon Beam took the opportunity to subtly rearrange the seating when he showed Jill Graham a diagram.

Body Language

Some people have a natural intuitive ability to establish rapport, while others struggle to feel natural at any time in an interview. Observing successful interviewers or conversationalists (at a party, for example) can give you some clues on achieving good rapport. Body language and verbal matching are covered in some detail in Chapter 9. Observers of human behaviour note that when a person 'matches' another person in behaviour, rapport results. This approach must be used naturally (nobody likes to be 'aped'). Ideally it occurs at a subconscious level so it happens without a conscious effort. This is more likely to happen if you, the interviewer, being well organized and well prepared, can relax and give your full attention and interest to the person you are about to interview. If you are worrying about making a good impression, or a spot of grease on your clothes, or an urgent telephone message, you are less likely to succeed. We all modify our behaviour and speech patterns to some extent when mixing with different groups of people. Think of what you are like on a night out with a group of friends, and compare that with how you act and talk if you invite your boss to dinner. Both experiences may well be enjoyable, but they will probably be very different. The key to success is to be **genuinely** interested in other people.

Control

It is important during an interview to maintain direction **and** to maintain control, but with subtlety. There may be times when important issues have not been foreseen and it is then your responsibility, as interviewer, to mentally consult your objectives, determine if the new information is necessary and, if not, to politely and skilfully redirect the discussion.

You also need to remember that people **will** ramble on from time to time. In the middle of an intense interview this can be valuable to give you a few moments to consolidate your thoughts and figure out which tack to take next. As in normal conversation, choose your moment to interrupt carefully and try to build on something the interviewee has just said to steer the conversation to something more relevant. For example, you can break in with a statement, such as: *"That sounds interesting – how does it relate to ... X ... ?"*, where ... X ... is something more directly relevant. Make sure that the linkage between what the interviewee is rambling about and ... X ... is reasonably clear, otherwise the interviewee may feel you are just plain rude.

Regaining control is illustrated when Gordon Beam finds Jill Graham drifting off the point:

	... she is clearly losing focus on the point and starting to ramble a little!
Gordon Beam (interrupting politely)	*"Yes, I can see that would be very useful to know. I am particularly interested in something you said earlier – about feedback from the local business community. I wonder whether there is any tangible way of measuring that?"*

To maintain control of the direction of the interview and be in command of the general topics, tact is essential. On the one hand, you do not want the interviewee to ramble unnecessarily but, on the other, you need to avoid talking too much yourself. As a general rule, the interviewer should aim to talk for about a fifth of the time in an interview: talk too much and the information gathered may be insufficient; talk too little and the direction and control of the interview may be less than ideal (or it may take longer than need be to get the right information).

Finally, it is important to remember to thank interviewees for their time and to keep them informed of future developments. This is just common courtesy, but it is surprisingly overlooked on occasions.

In closing an interview, take the opportunity to confirm future meetings, such as feedback sessions or second interviews. This helps to co-ordinate the dates and to gain the interviewee's commitment to attend. The ending of the interview between Gordon Beam, Alan Scott and Jill Graham shows a good technique for closing an interview.

> *"Well, thank you for giving us so much of your time this morning, Jill. We will work on these ideas and directions, plus any others we pick up over the next week or so, and we will try to devise a consolidated set of objectives and facilities for the feedback meeting in six weeks' time ..."*

Consolidation

Using the Information

Just as time is required for preparation before the interview, time is also required afterwards to review notes and tapes made during it, to review any documents collected, and to compile the information to be used from that interview.

Try to schedule time for consolidation as soon as possible after the actual interview, when it is still fresh in your minds. The interviewer and the note-taker may have picked up somewhat different signals from their interviewee, and there may indeed be two sets of notes to consolidate. Although the bulk of writing will have been done by the note-taker, the interviewer may have added to or annotated the initial checklist during the interview. At this point, add any extra comments to your notes and then review and mark the notes to obtain the information you require in order to support the specific objectives of the interview. It is useful to create a follow-up list if there are a number of interviews. One technique is to post the list in the project room. If you have used a tape recorder, you may want to review highly detailed sections of the taped interview and add the detail to your notes.

An interview will often uncover facts and ideas that are useful to the overall project but not directly relevant to the reason for the particular interview that has generated this additional information. The discussion during the interview causes creative thought, especially in the note-taker who, if any good, will record these ideas. For example, for a project involving information systems development, some imaginative ideas may have come out about the system design which would be useful later on in the development life cycle. These should be noted and marked for possible use in the future.

The amount of time invested and the form of the consolidation should be in line with the purpose. In our example, Gordon Beam is going to use the information from the interview with Jill Graham to direct his initial attempts at developing a blueprint for a new hotel. Together with Alan Scott, he may highlight key objectives, issues and ideas and then use these as a checklist after Scott does some early design work on the hotel itself.

A description of several techniques used for a structured analysis of the notes is given in Chapter 8. One useful technique is to identify in the notes certain key elements; for example, drawing boxes around business objectives, underscoring business functions and circling important information items (entities). An experienced note-taker will often perform quite a lot of consolidation during the interview itself.

Usually, the information gained from one or more interviews will be used for some specified purpose. Common examples include:

- resolving business problems and issues
- developing agreed business strategies
- redesigning business processes
- acting as the basis from which to design business systems
- reviewing the applicability of existing business systems.

Summary

So, an interview can be seen as having three distinct phases:

- Preparation, with all the planning, allocation of roles, scheduling, and so on, to make sure that the right people are in the right place at the right time. This is possibly the most important phase, and one frequently undervalued by novice interviewers. Don't forget *"time spent in reconnaissance is never wasted"*.

- Then there is conducting the interview, during which it falls to the interviewer to keep a controlled conversation going, in order to achieve a purpose, while the note-taker scribbles away (often frantically) to keep up – recording the relevant information.

- Finally, making use of the information gained, as a start (or in addition) to structured modelling and your team understanding of what is going on and as a springboard to preparation for subsequent interviews.

Figure 3-4
Summary of Basic Techniques

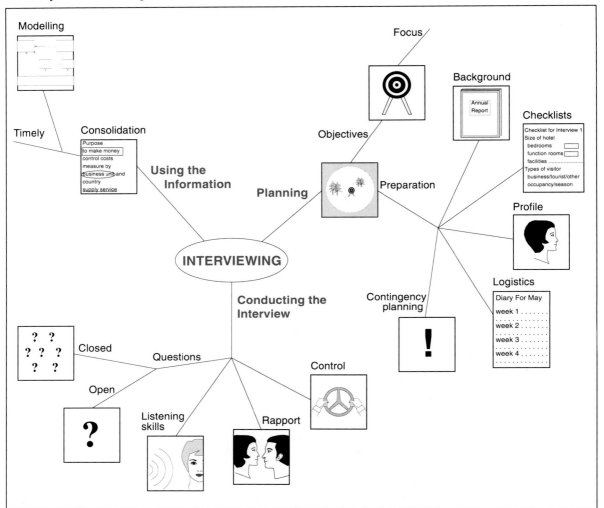

Chapter

4

GETTING THE FEEL FOR INTERVIEWING

Introduction

This short chapter looks at some fairly painless ways to try out a few of the key skills needed for conducting a successful interview. There is no doubt that the most effective way to learn how to interview is to 'do it for real'. Practise the techniques in a real but controlled situation – make mistakes and learn from them. The alternative of reading this book and then diving into your first, critical, senior-level interview is risky!

Four Key Skills

A top-class interviewer requires many skills, but in this chapter we will focus on the four basic skills of open questioning, active listening, note-taking and observation and suggest ways in which you can practise them safely in everyday situations. Once you have read the chapter we hope you will work through the examples to gain **practical** experience of how it feels to use these interviewing techniques.

If you are new to interviewing, practise these basic skills and become proficient before taking on an ambitious or critical interviewing role. If you are already a proficient interviewer, it may still be useful to step back and refresh a basic skill.

Open Questioning

An open question is one that cannot be answered with a 'yes', 'no' or short factual answer. For example:

> *"Tell me about the essence of your business as you see it."*

> *"How do you determine success or failure in your company?"*

> *"What is it like to work for your company?"*

Everyday Conversation

Fortunately, everyday conversation with family, friends and colleagues is an excellent opportunity for using the questioning technique. A family meal, a social event, booking a holiday, all provide good chances to practise this skill. Open questions are useful for gathering information, so look for an opening in the conversation to ask for someone's opinion or some information about a particular topic. At a party, for example, if people are discussing their plans for the next summer vacation or recounting past experiences there should be plenty of opportunities.

If your natural conversational style is didactic, you like to tell other people things and contribute your ideas rather than inquire about their ideas (you are a talker rather than a listener), this conscious use of open questioning may feel odd and uncomfortable at first. If, however, your natural style inclines towards inquiry, it should be much easier for you. In any case, we recommend using just one or two open questions in the conversation at first, gradually (possibly over a number of days) working up to a stage where you can comfortably switch in and out of open questioning mode at will.

The Unwary Traveller

Are you sitting next to someone on a plane or a train? If so, perhaps a friendly, open question would pass a few minutes harmlessly. Or you could try one out when you are in a queue waiting to be served in a bank or a shop. And if you make a bit of a hash if it at first, take comfort in the thought that you will probably never see the person again anyway!

Part of this chapter was written while on a plane. The author, who was sitting next to a pilot, asked a classic closed question as they took their seats: *"I bet it feels strange being a passenger rather than the pilot?"* The pilot grunted something non-committal and nodded, and that was the end of that. The response might have been rather more constructive to the open question: *"What's it like to be a passenger rather than the pilot?"*

Another Interviewer

One great opportunity to experiment with open questions under controlled circumstances is to find and then interview another interviewer, especially if the other interviewer is an expert, in which case you should be able to get some professional hints and tips at the same time. Topics you could discuss include:

- the other person's hobby or family or job
- a recent sporting or other topical event
- food and wine
- or, if you are really ambitious, an interview on interviewing.

Make sure you choose a topic the other person is both familiar with and interested in. This should make it easier, as most people talk very freely once you get them started on a favourite subject.

Which brings us to the second basic skill.

Active Listening

Active listening is the ability to hear and **understand** what is said and to reflect that understanding by way of brief summaries from time to time. Clearly, social and family events can again be used as an opportunity to practise a technique. There is little point in asking open questions if you are not prepared to listen to the answers!

News Broadcasts

Television and radio news broadcasts are a good source for active listening. Try listening to a portion of a broadcast and making summary statements (speak them out aloud if you are on your own). Do not make the summaries too frequent – no more than one every couple of minutes or so – and look for natural breaks to make them. Of course, there is no reaction to your summary from the broadcaster (who will carry on talking anyway) but this situation has the advantage that you can practise in private. When you are feeling confident with your skill you can move on to a more public situation.

Telephone Calls

Sometimes people can be distracted from the task of listening by the presence of the interviewee, especially by eye contact and body language. Active listening can be practised easily and naturally in an ordinary telephone call. Try the phrase *"... so, what you are saying is ..."*, followed by your summary of what you think the person on the other end of the phone has just said. Keep this short and relevant, using your own words rather than repeating what the other person has said (in contrast to the note-taking exercise below, where noting exactly what is said in the other person's terms is key). This is, of course, a good general conversational technique not limited to interviewing.

Note the response that you get to your summary. If it is a good summary you will give the other person confidence that you have understood and may receive an enthusiastic *"yes, yes, that's exactly right"*. At other times, your summary may spark off related thoughts and you may get a qualified *"well no, not quite, when I said everyone, I really meant all the people I saw last week ..."*. Occasionally (if you have misunderstood or summarized poorly) the response will be a negative *"Oh no! not at all, I meant ..."*, often in an exasperated tone of voice that indicates that the listener feels you have **not** listened carefully. It is better to experience this type of response with a friend or colleague than in front of an important interviewee.

Most people enjoy talking on the telephone, especially if someone else pays the bill for a long call, but a few normally talkative people are unusually brusque on the telephone. You may feel it best to avoid practising your skills on them. Or perhaps you will see them as a challenge as you become proficient.

Note-taking

Note-taking is the third key skill. The main point in good note-taking is to take accurate notes of the main, relevant statements, noting the terms that the interviewee uses.

Chat Shows, Newscasts and TV Interviews

These broadcasts provide a good opportunity for taking notes. Again, focus on the key points and try to note their meaning. Note-taking is all about trying to capture the meaning, tone and **terms** used by the interviewee succinctly. In particular, concentrate on using the terms that the speaker is using; do not filter them and use your own terms instead.

Do not be too disheartened if you find this exercise difficult. Newscasts, for example, are edited and may impart a huge amount of information in a short space of time. If you are taking notes on something that has already been précised, you may find your notes are almost as long as the original. On the other hand, a large proportion of what is said is relevant and worth recording. Live chat shows and interviews may be less taxing on the writing hand, but will need more careful sifting to pick out the key points from the general conversation.

In a televised interview, also study the interviewer's style – can you spot the techniques being used? This brings us to the final key skill.

Observation

Being aware of what is really happening in an interview is very important. This involves not just the obvious things, such as what is said and any diagrams and notes that are drawn up, but less obvious signals like tone of voice, facial expressions, hand and head movements. Take a step back from the active interviewing skills you have been practising to study closely some conversations in any of the previously mentioned settings. Consider what you can tell from:

- what is said
- the tone of voice used
- the volume at which it is said
- facial expressions
- body movements, such as hand gestures, nodding of heads, leaning forward or backward
- use of other items, such as playing with a pen top or doodling on scraps of paper.

Compare and contrast what you see and hear in meetings at work, customers interacting with sales assistants in shops, your family and friends conversing together – any situation involving a conversation between two people or a group of people, for example, at a party. The purpose of taking a little time out to consider these interactions more closely is to become aware that there is plenty of meaning communicated, apart from what is actually said! There is a chapter on non-verbal communication later in the book, but for now try observing a few conversations to become familiar with the way people talk to one another in practice.

Acquiring New Skills

Many of the skills and techniques of successful interviewing rely on your **behaving** in a certain way. Learning to ask open questions and to listen actively may require a change in your own behaviour and observation depends on your awareness of other people's behaviour. If this style of behaviour is new to you (or at least different from your natural style) then adopting it and becoming proficient will take some time and practice.

When learning a series of new skills and techniques, it is best to introduce new behaviour gradually, changing one thing at a time. Try adopting an open questioning technique over a period of several days. Recognize that you will make mistakes, criticize yourself, and make improvements until you feel natural and comfortable and able to switch in and out of the technique at will. Experience what it feels like – you may be quite surprised by the response you get from others, especially if you normally tend to do most of the talking.

Having become proficient at one new behaviour, you can take on a second. You may find that it takes quite a while to become comfortable with the second new technique because you will be conscious of how it is the combination and the interrelation of techniques that is so important. As you adopt more techniques the interaction becomes more complex. If you start with open questioning and progress to active listening, as your listening skills improve you will want to hone your questioning skills further. As your powers of observation develop, you will find your observations help you to frame better questions and 'hear' more accurately. You will be able to note the way things are said, or perhaps left unsaid, rather than simply the actual words spoken.

Learning to interview is like learning to drive. You can learn the skills about using the pedals, and the gears, and the steering, and observing the road fairly easily one at a time. Putting it all together takes a little longer.

Chapter

5

INTERVIEW PREPARATION

Introduction

The success of any interview depends upon good advance preparation, which often begins before any formal meeting between the project team and the project sponsor. In this chapter, we look at techniques used to prepare for an interview. Initially, we discuss the briefing session and informal investigative work that can be done before a project gets under way, and then the remaining part of the chapter looks at the preparation involved for an individual interview.

A Typical Project

A medium-sized manufacturing company is updating its financial and stock-handling systems. As this entails new computer hardware, software and probably quite a lot of staff training, the company has decided that this is a suitable time to examine its overall information-handling strategy. We need to build up a picture of everything that goes on in the company, or should be going on, and why.

On the first day at the main site, we take a tour of the key areas with one of the 'old-timers' who knows about the people and activities there. Having observed the factory operations for many years, his knowledge and side comments will be of great interest, although they are likely to be subjective. Experience, however, tells us to listen for reasons to explain his comments; sometimes the reasons are of general application. After touring the main site we are taken on a brief tour of other sites. All of this gives us a broad impression of how things are done, who works with whom, the flow of activities and the scale of the total enterprise.

Our next step is to sit down with the sponsor of our project and to look over the organization charts and determine who should be interviewed and why. As we discuss the interviewee list, we are checking possibilities against our objective of obtaining a high-level strategic understanding of the organization – so we need to talk to representative senior managers to achieve that objective.

We draw up a list of twelve first-round interviews with members of staff responsible for various areas, including finance, sales, production and major product lines. Establishing the whole list at the same time, with some leeway for extra interviews, allows us to set up an interview plan for the information-gathering phase of the project. This needs to be done well in advance to ensure the possibility of fitting everyone into the schedule. We often find that senior-level staff are especially busy and may be away from their offices for long periods, so it is realistic to plan several weeks in advance. In this case, we have a scheduling constraint as one of the product directors is leaving soon on a trip to China.

Taking another example from our ongoing story of Atlantis Island Flights:

Site Tour for the Hotel Project

At the Board Meeting in March, the go-ahead is given for the project. The objectives are to provide travellers with comfortable easy-to-use facilities while staying in Atlantis and to provide conference, meeting and entertainment facilities for the island in general.

Before introducing Gordon Beam, the consultant, at a briefing session, Jill Graham arranges an informal tour of the proposed site for Beam, members of the Board, and other interested airline staff. The one-hundred-acre site close to the airport was acquired for the airline ten years previously by Lawrence Parker with an arrangement that the farmer could continue to farm the land until it was required. This tour involves some time being spent with the farmer, which proves useful as his local knowledge adds to what the inspection reports and maps of the area have revealed. He is able to comment on the state of the land (drainage, fertility, and so on) and where the best views and access routes can be found. From listening to the conversation amongst the various members of the group, a picture starts to emerge of each individual's perception of the project. (Pete Stirling makes it very clear that he is worried it will all cost too much!)

Jill also approaches some local businesses in order to gauge their initial reactions to some of the ideas proposed. Most of the reactions are positive, strengthening her hopes for a smooth and successful project.

Briefing Meeting

An early introduction to the area of a business being studied helps to achieve a level of broad understanding, providing a context in which to hold an initial briefing session. This is essential on any large project. Within the first few days of a project, where interviews will be an important part of the information gathering, a briefing meeting attended by all the interviewees is usually arranged.

The briefing meeting is held in order to answer the who, why, what, when and how questions the participants in the project are likely to have. One important aspect is that this meeting builds enthusiasm and commitment to the project and, generally, an hour and a half is long enough. (American football fans sometimes refer to this briefing as a 'kick-off' meeting.)

A typical agenda helps to show how the different elements of a briefing meeting are developed:

Agenda	
1. Introductions and team members	– getting to know who is who
2. Background of project and current situation	– recap of why we are all here
3. Examples of deliverables	– what the project is aiming to produce
4. Method of working/approach	– how we will go about producing the deliverables
5. Project plan/what will be done	– when it will all happen
6. Discussion of expectations and questions	– a chance to voice any remaining concerns and issues

The list of interviewees largely forms the list of those to invite to attend the briefing meeting. In a strategic project the meeting is usually at board level, held in the board room or a similar conference room, and scheduled to last approximately one and a half hours. The agenda above illustrates the coverage for a strategy study. The last point is crucial: providing time for questions and asking about expectations for the project helps to open important channels of communication and understanding.

We usually like to assemble everyone involved in a project (or as many as is practical) right at the start to set the scene and let people know what to expect (and what is expected of them!). Usually this means asking senior executives **not** to prepare for their interviews in advance but to react to questions at the time, since we are looking for ideas, opinions and a degree of emotional commitment which can easily be disguised in a prepared interview.

Briefing meetings brief both interviewers and interviewees.

The meeting also provides an opportunity to observe the dynamics and interaction of the future interviewees as a group. Important observations about the culture and about the management and leadership style can be made at this time. Authoritarian cultures, for example, are easy to identify: everyone waits for the most senior person to take charge and express opinions, and similar deferential actions surface. This may occur in spite of contrary statements about intended style in the organization. A briefing meeting usually provides an initial political map. Negative queries can serve to make known anyone who may be wary of the project.

We can recall a meeting where no one spoke until the Managing Director spoke. And there was a project where everyone had a scheduled interview appointment except the top manager who was 'too busy'. At the end of the briefing, however, he was the first to sign up for an actual appointment – for that same afternoon. He cleared his diary immediately for a four-hour interview, convinced that it was important for us to talk with him first.

Briefing Session for the Hotel Project

Lawrence Parker opens the briefing meeting with a short address during which he gives the reasons for building a hotel and then Jill Graham takes over the running of the meeting. She introduces the project team, Gordon Beam and his associates. She spends half an hour explaining, in a little more detail, the goals they are trying to achieve, which include:

- *building a top-quality hotel that meets local, high, environmental standards*
- *gaining the lion's share of local conference business*
- *improving facilities for the non-tourist community*
- *providing sporting and leisure facilities*

– and, of course, adding to the profitability and future prosperity of the airline itself.

She finally gives some idea of the project timescales before handing over to Gordon Beam. He explains that they aim to get everyone to contribute their own ideas and preferences individually, leaving the project team to consolidate them all and try to produce an overall design for the hotel that they can all agree upon. He also assures the group that there will be a feedback session held after the individual interviews, at which time they can comment on and modify the proposals being made. To give people an example of what to expect, he talks through the results of a similar project he completed last year.

Jill closes the meeting with an open invitation to ask questions. Most of the negative queries, regarding long-term financial planning, are voiced by Pete Stirling and his team. On the whole, however, the response is positive, with Chris Hayley being especially enthusiastic.

After attending a good briefing session, the participants should be left with the feeling that they know what is expected of them and also what they can expect to see as a result of a project.

Copies of the presentation materials for the briefing meeting can be distributed in a folder to attendees and also given later to anyone who could not attend the briefing session itself. After the meeting it is useful to send out a letter to all the interviewees confirming the aims and objectives of the project, its scope and asking for their co-operation. Although it may be useful to refer to these during an interview, neither the conclusions from the briefing meeting nor the content of the follow-up letter are 'writ in stone'. They do not prevent reviews of project goals, nor do they assume that no further questions need to be asked. Let us now take a look at various aspects of planning a series of interviews as part of a large project.

Aims and Objectives

If you don't know where you are going, how will you know when you get there?

Aims and objectives are the means of providing us with an end-point, keeping us on that track and guiding a project towards a conclusion. They are the means of providing a focus for an interview. A clear set of aims and objectives makes it possible to decide whether an interview is straying too far from the point and will help to ensure that the right information is forthcoming. We have explored the aims and objectives of interviewing in some depth in Chapter 3. The first step in preparation is to define your aims and objectives in order to direct you in the next stages of interview planning – deciding who to interview.

Planning

The Interview List

Who should be on the list? The answer to this question depends entirely upon the objectives you have set and the type of information you require. In an enterprise-wide study, for example, the sponsor of the project can help the interviewers determine the candidates. The most common problem is to have more names suggested than time available – look out for repetitive information gathering that takes time away from other tasks. There is a quick drop-off in the new information acquired in successive interviews. By recognizing that fact early, it is possible to make the most out of fewer in-depth interviews. About seven to ten in-depth, senior-level interviews are usually sufficient for strategic information gathering.

Figure 5-1
Value of Adding
One More Interview

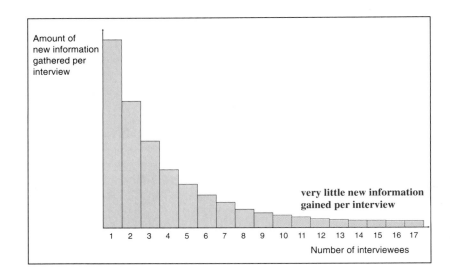

So Who **Should** Be on the List?

Let's interview everyone! – no, that will take too long. Just Ethel? – she's the expert on the subject – no, there can be no credibility in just having a single viewpoint; besides, she might be wrong! So if it is not everyone and it is not just Ethel, how do we decide?

This conversation has been held many times by project teams setting up interviews. The dilemma is usually resolved by determining the time available and following the recommendations of the project sponsor or someone knowledgeable about the people in the organization. Let us take a look at a few things that can help you to decide.

Subject Coverage

Not everyone will know all there is to know about a given subject – generally, each individual in an organization understands a certain area in depth and a wider area at a more superficial level.

If you work with a sponsor, after a quick chat with a few senior people, possibly at a briefing session, you can rapidly build up a picture of who would be expert on specific subjects. You can use an organization chart showing 'who's who' in the area you are interested in and ask them to identify the key people. Circle their names to indicate their main expertise and areas of wider but less detailed knowledge. This will help you to decide who has in-depth understanding of various topics and who has good general understanding that would be useful for cross-checking after other interviews. It will also help you avoid too many interviews of people whose expertise overlaps or is very narrow.

In the example of the manufacturing company, we decide to interview the entire Board of Directors as each is responsible for a key functional area and most have many years of practical experience at the plant. The one exception is a new Finance Director, who encourages us to include an additional interviewee to obtain more complete financial information.

When choosing interviewees to achieve coverage of a subject area, look for people that:

- are responsible for an area
- have personal experience
- have been recommended by others for their personal expertise
- will be interested and supportive of your information gathering.

Detailed interviews may be driven by business processes or business functions. The task of selecting interviewees can, therefore, be structured around the 'doers' who are responsible for some subset of the business activities, including technical and operations staff and information technology specialists and auditors, as well as managers. It may be useful to draw up a matrix of business functions against people to ensure that the right scope is covered during the interviews. The matrix can then be used to decide whom to interview and what types of questions to ask.

For example, Figure 5-2 below shows a part of this matrix for Atlantis Island Flights which covers issuing tickets to passengers and checking them in for their flights. Gordon Beam needs to learn more about the sale of tickets and how this particular process could operate in the future, especially in relation to clients who want to make a hotel reservation at the same time. In this instance, he finds he needs to interview Joe Black, the Ticket Sales Manager, and Jeremy Adams, the Reservations Manager, to gain a clear insight into the way things work. These two interviews will also serve as a useful cross-check to interviews focusing on other subjects that Black and Adams know about, such as maintaining standard fares.

Figure 5-2
Part of a Business Function to Person Matrix

Business Functions	Parker	Singer	Evans	Black	Graham	Adams	Stirling	Slater	Fernandez	Schwartz	Cheng	van Velden	Hayley	Tracey
Establish schedule of flight														✓
Issue ticket for passenger*				✓		✓								
Check person in for flight*						✓								
Maintain standard fares	✓		✓	✓		✓	✓				✓			
Place advertising e.g. in newspaper		✓	✓											
Train staff							✓						✓	
Inspect/repair aircraft							✓	✓	✓	✓				
Refuel aircraft								✓	✓					

* priority from Strategy Stage

Scope is important for interviews searching for detailed information, as both breadth and depth are required. It is necessary to identify interviewees who are at an appropriate level of the organization, in order that they can communicate awareness of business objectives while having a knowledge of day-to-day procedures and problems; that is, they know what **really** happens in practice.

Position in the Organization

Organizations differ in the way they treat the authority given to a position in the management structure and cross-departmental communication. Sometimes there are unwritten rules that imply you cannot interview a person without interviewing that person's manager. In other organizations, a free 'you can talk to anyone about anything' ruling may exist.

At Atlantis Island Flights, the International Operations Director, Joe Tracey, feels quite strongly that he should grant permission for any member of his team to be interviewed. However, on one occasion Gordon Beam happens to meet a key member of staff at lunch and discusses some details of the project with him. The following day Joe Tracey asks Jill Graham to come into his office in order to justify this unscheduled meeting and demands to know what Gordon has been told by the expert!

Maybe this is an unusual case, but it pays to know the right protocol for getting things done on a project. It often turns out that people are sensitive to allowing members of their staff to participate without being interviewed themselves, so it may be that an interview with a line manager is needed before interviewing members of staff who are knowledgeable about a particular subject.

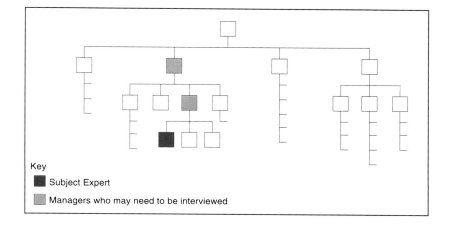

Key
■ Subject Expert
▨ Managers who may need to be interviewed

Interviews with direct line managers of subject experts can be relatively short and will probably yield little new information, but they should be handled with care. For example:

"We know you are very busy, so we will keep this interview short and to the point."

"Whom would you recommend we talk to if we need detailed descriptions on this area?"

"We've been warned you have another appointment at 3.00 p.m., so we will ensure we finish by then."

Interviewing for Courtesy

Interviews of people by virtue of their position in the organization rather than their specific knowledge or expertise are really courtesy interviews. They can, however, serve several purposes. First, they satisfy diplomatic niceties and respect protocol rather than discover new information, but they may also be useful for cross-checking perspectives or policies at different levels. Although you should only need to select two or three of them, allow for additional interviews which may be suggested as in-depth interviewing progresses. It can be a useful tactic to set up interviews with people of influence who would not otherwise be interviewed but who are opposed to the project. Be careful not to miss out people who may feel they should be involved because their colleagues are being interviewed.

**Figure 5-4
Example of a
Courtesy Interview**

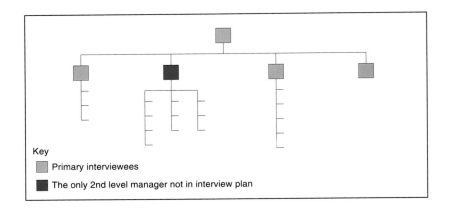

Key

□ Primary interviewees

■ The only 2nd level manager not in interview plan

Interviewing in Groups

The possibility of interviewing more than one person in a single interview is occasionally mooted. The question may be raised when schedules are being drawn up and suggestions to 'double up' or to meet in small groups are put forward. In general, for the purpose of information gathering, you obtain the most candid information with only one interviewee at a time. Although group interviews may sometimes be appropriate, there is a real danger that you will obtain less information and achieve less rapport when more than one person is included in the same interview.

We have observed different cultural views on this topic in international consulting and believe that the interview team needs to be sensitive and skilful in communicating the reasons for a general rule of one interviewee at a time. It may be perceived as threatening in some cultures to be 'questioned' in a solo interview. In other cultural settings the importance of the meeting may be judged by how many people attend, so an interview with only one person is not considered important. The focus on the goal of information gathering, in contrast to conventional meetings, must be clearly stated and understood by everyone involved, including those engaged in the scheduling process, the interviewees and all project team members. For group interviews to be successful, interviewing skills also need to be supplemented by facilitator and group management skills.

Different Types of Interview

In most projects the pressure to have a talk with many people is very real, but it is important to agree guidelines for selecting interviewees at the outset. Some interviewers find it helpful to arrange one set of interviews for information gathering and other, shorter, interviews for political and organizational reasons. One of the managers, for example, may be new to the job and unlikely to be able to give you the sort of detailed information you need. The solution is to plan a brief visit to the new manager but schedule a longer interview with the most experienced person in that area. The main point is to distinguish between the reasons and objectives for the interviews and to plan the time and interviewees accordingly.

Senior In-depth Interview

The interviewee here is likely to be very senior in the organization. The purpose of the interview is to gather advice and direction on a fairly wide scope and is generally conducted early in a project. Typically hard to plan, because of executives with busy schedules, you often get one chance only at this type of interview – so make sure it is a success. It is best to plan only one of these interviews in any one day.

A template for planning purposes is given below with two elapsed days allotted to each interview. By scheduling the interview for the morning, the interviewer can be available for the whole day if the meeting is extended. More likely, the busy executive will need extra time flexibility. In this event, you can consolidate the first interview the following morning and still have ample time to prepare for the next interview.

	a.m.		p.m.	
Mon				Mon
Tues			Prepare 1	Tues
Wed	Interview 1		Consolidate 1	Wed
Thur			Prepare 2	Thur
Fri				Fri
Sat				Sat
Sun				Sun

Fact-finding Interview

This type of interview is primarily to uncover facts and figures on one or more specific points. For example, with regard to the dining facilities at the proposed hotel on Atlantis, this information will include the quantities of food that need to be ordered and when, who the suppliers will be, what facilities there are for storage, and so on. These interviews are typically held with people closer to the day-to-day operations in a business and are often scheduled after a project has been running for some time and a reasonable understanding of the business has already been built up by the project team. Up to three fact-finding interviews are possible per day per interviewer, although care should be taken to avoid having too many of them crammed end to end as this can lead to a very inflexible schedule – things **do** go wrong and interviews need to be rescheduled!

The template for planning this type of interview shows two interviews per day, but preparation and consolidation are also completed in the same day.

	a.m.		p.m.
Mon			
Tues	Prepare 1 Interview 1 Consolidate 1		Prepare 2 Interview 2 Consolidate 2
Wed			
Thur			

Courtesy Interviews

As these are necessary for political, diplomatic or procedural reasons and are likely to yield very little factual information, they can be scheduled to last under an hour each, with a few minutes preparation beforehand. Three or four interviews are possible in a single day.

Casual Interview

Finally, information on a single specific topic or clarification of a point of contention may be needed. In this case, a telephone call or a brief meeting can be arranged. An opportunity may also arise if you encounter someone on a casual basis, so it is helpful to keep one or two such points in mind.

For instance, on the Atlantis project, Gordon Beam bumps into Mandy Evans, the Agent Liaison Officer, at the coffee machine, while waiting to see Jill Graham, and Mandy asks how the project is going. *"Really well,"* says Gordon. *"We have finished most of the interviews now and we're trying to clear up a few loose ends – actually, you might be able to help me there – do you think there would be any security implications with having boarding cards issued in the hotel?"*

Scheduling

It is likely that all these types of interview – senior in-depth, fact-finding and courtesy – will be necessary during a project. The time allocated for each type is based on the purpose and objectives of the interview and should not be easily compromised by pressure from budget holders, tight timescales or interviewees. In most organizations there always seems to be a crisis brewing, which tugs at senior management's and experts' time.

One of the key distinctions between a social conversation and a business interview is the level of planning required. Most social conversations are spontaneous or only generally planned around a topic of mutual interest. In contrast, an interview often requires careful planning in order to obtain the necessary information during the time available. Many of the problems and pitfalls of interviewing can be avoided by careful planning.

Making mistakes is part of the learning process, as Kevin found when he was given his first project to run. Unfortunately, he had not been too careful when planning the interviews and ended up cramming ten into one week, to be carried out by two people and with no contingency. A problem with the first interview caused it to overrun; the second interviewee, who was based at a different office a couple of miles away, cancelled when the team failed to turn up after ten minutes. (They were still making their way between sites.) This interview had to be rescheduled after the irate manager, who was known for his 'short fuse', was placated. The cumulative effect of careless planning and the lack of contingency was that there was insufficient time to consolidate the interviews and the danger, narrowly avoided in this instance, that the manager who is not interviewed objects strongly to how he has been treated and blocks the project conclusions.

The following table gives some indication of the scheduling requirements for different types of interview.

	Interviewer	Note-taker	Preparation Time	Interview Time	Consolidation
In-depth*	✓✓	✓✓	3–4 hours	3–4 hours	3–4 hours
Fact-finding	✓✓	✓	1 hour	1–2 hours	1 hour
Courtesy	✓	✓	½ hour	1 hour	½ hour
Casual	✓✓	X	–	minutes	minutes
Group workshop*	✓✓	✓✓	4 hours–1 day	4 hours–1 day	4 hours

Table Key

✓✓   definitely needed
✓   useful, but can manage without
X   not useful
*   third person as an observer or 'flywheel' may be useful (see page 63)

It is important to allow sufficient time between interviews for consolidation, but it is also necessary to plan with a degree of flexibility, so that changes in the schedule can be accommodated as priorities in people's lives change.

You may remember that Pete Stirling, the Financial Director of Atlantis Island Flights, was sceptical about the hotel project right from the start. His co-operation, however, is essential to start the ball rolling smoothly financially, so Jill Graham, Gordon Beam and their team decide to tackle him early on! After all, if they can get him in agreement, it will make life an awful lot easier. They feel that it is best if Jill takes no part in this interview, so Gordon assigns one of his own non-airline staff to the role of note-taker and he takes the interviewing role himself.

The interview is arranged for the beginning of May and Gordon is feeling pretty confident. Then he has the first of a series of set-backs.

"Sorry, Pete is unwell today – he won't be in the office."

"I hope he feels better soon – let's make another date – not free until the end of May! – oh well, not ideal, but let's go with it."

The interview at the end of May is cancelled as important clients fly in at the last moment, so a new date is set for mid-June. Unfortunately, Pete has to cancel once again as he wishes to attend a financial conference on the mainland and cannot get back in time. The meeting finally takes place at the end of June, much to Gordon's relief (and Jill's too), but only a week before the feedback session is due to take place.

Many people are very surprised when interviews of four hours are suggested for strategic-level or senior in-depth interviewing. Comments such as *"no one will give us that much time"* or *"what will we discuss for that long?"* are common. However, experience shows that:

- it actually **is possible** to obtain four hours of executive time if there is a belief that it is worthwhile
- four hours is necessary for exploration of strategic-level issues.

We have often scheduled **additional** time with senior executives, at their request, following a successful interview.

Once the interview list has been produced and all the interviews scheduled, you need to provide this information to everyone on the project. One format that is useful and can be posted on the project room wall, along with an organization chart, is shown in the schedule opposite. A project administrator is normally responsible for keeping track of such a schedule – making sure rooms are booked, rebooking when things change, ensuring sufficient contingency arrangements exist in case something goes wrong, and so on. This should not stop the interviewing team from checking the arrangements themselves, just to be absolutely certain.

Interview Schedule						
Date	**Interviewee Name**	**Job Title**	**Location**	**Contact Number**	**Interviewer Note-taker Observer**	**Booked by**
01/05	Lawrence Parker	Chief Executive Officer	his office	7135	Gordon Beam Jill Graham	Jill Graham
04/05	Pete Stirling	Chief Financial Officer	Meeting Room 3	7140	Gordon Beam Steve Williams Michelle Yves	Gordon Beam
08/05	Ed Singer	Sales & Marketing Director	his office	7138	Jill Graham Gordon Beam	Jill Graham

The success of an interview is closely related to the degree of planning, which includes:

- Allocation of time – in the overall planning process make sure there is sufficient time to prepare for the interview, to carry it out and to consolidate the information gained.

- Sequence of interviews – have the senior, direction-setting interviews early in the project.

- Planning the objectives – what is the purpose of each interview?

- Contingency plans – in case things do not go according to plan.

Location

With the interviewees selected and the scheduling begun, the next part of planning is to consider the site of the interviews. Do you go to the offices or the work areas of the interviewees or do they come to a project room? The recommendation is usually to hold an interview at the normal work area of the interviewee because arrangements can then be made to visit and tour a site. It also has the advantage of reference materials being more readily available. An interviewee may refer to a report he uses to measure the progress of some activity – in his own office, he is more likely to have a copy to hand to show you. Being at the interviewee's normal work area also allows the interviewer to observe the natural working atmosphere and culture. Disadvantages include the possibility of interruptions and lack of privacy. If more than one person is being interviewed at the same time, a conference room is generally more suitable.

Interviewing Team

Generally speaking, the type of interview to be conducted determines the interview team that is set up. The most common team, however, consists of two people – the interviewer and the note-taker. The person with the most interviewing experience usually takes the role of interviewer, but if one person has more specific industry experience than the other (process engineering or flexible manufacturing, for example) then it is worth considering using that person as the interviewer when there will be a high technical content in the interview.

In one situation, a relatively new member of the interviewing team who normally took the role of note-taker had an engineering background. Mary took the role of interviewer for technical interviews, and sometimes switched into this role for parts of other interviews, where her knowledge of the specialized vocabulary and understanding of the underlying engineering concepts enabled her to conduct the interview in more depth. But good analysts and experienced interviewers are skilled in probing new areas and the skills of the interviewer often outweigh technical knowledge in obtaining good interview material.

Multilingual Projects

In international situations, local language may be a consideration in selecting roles – the person with the best language skills may be able to conduct the interview in a second language. When an interpreter is available, it is better to choose the most experienced interviewer, even if the note-taker has some language ability. The higher quality of the questioning will yield the best information.

Language issues need to be confronted in the planning phase because time to prepare the interpreter should to be included in the scheduling. The most important preparation for an interpreter is a briefing on the objectives of the interview, so that the interpreter can actively assist and also determine if specialist vocabulary may be used during the interview. One of the difficulties in dual-language interviews is the translation of specialized terms. In the financial field, relatively straightforward terms such as 'accounts receivable' and 'accounts payable' are often a stumbling block for generally fluent translators. Preparation in advance with a list of special terms helps avoid confusion during the actual interview.

The Interviewer

The interviewer's role is to keep the conversation flowing and to control the topics covered, especially if the interviewee tends to ramble or drift back to the same topic all the time. Specifically, the interviewer needs good interpersonal skills in the areas of questioning and listening actively and an ability to handle controlled intervention (we will return to these in Chapter 6, "Conducting a Business Interview").

The Note-taker	The note-taker's role is to capture all the information offered by the interviewee in a form that can be used by the project afterwards and to support the interviewer by asking clarification and follow-up questions. In Chapter 7 more detail will be given on the specific tasks of the note-taker but, at the planning stage, we are concerned with assigning people as note-takers for scheduling purposes. As you select people for the roles, take the following into consideration:

- for an interviewer, look for someone who:
  - is personable
  - is a good communicator
  - is quick thinking
  - is experienced in the appropriate type of interviewing
  - has the ability to grasp new ideas quickly
  - is empathetic
  - demonstrates presence with the appropriate level of interviewee
  - and is experienced in the relevant industry.

- for a note-taker, look for someone who is:
  - a good listener
  - open (records what is said, not what he/she personally thinks)
  - patient
  - detail oriented
  - able to write legibly
  - able to model using structured techniques.

Solo Interview	There are situations where keeping a conversation going is not as important as in other types of interview and only one person is required to conduct the interview. For instance, with detailed fact-finding or hypothesis-testing (a situation designed to prove, or disprove, a particular belief), one person can play the roles of both interviewer and note-taker.

More than Two	There may be occasions when the interviewee is uncommunicative or there is trouble in keeping the conversation running smoothly; perhaps there is a clash of personality. In circumstances such as these, it can be useful for the interviewer and note-taker to swap roles or for a third person acting as a flywheel to be introduced. A flywheel in an interview has the same function as a flywheel in a piece of machinery – to keep things moving smoothly and iron out the surges and troughs, mainly the troughs, in the conversation. This is usually achieved by staying quietly out of the way when conservation is flowing, unless the interviewer needs help, and then stepping in with questions, observations, parallels from personal experience, and so on, to keep the event alive.

Back to the Atlantis Project

During the majority of the initial interviews on the hotel project, Gordon Beam decides to take on the role of interviewer himself. However, for the interview with Joe Tracey, he feels it prudent to include a flywheel. Tracey is the manager with the 'talk to any of my staff' attitude who nonetheless gets very upset when he finds out that Gordon has met one of his staff at lunch and conducted a casual interview – they talked business over lunch!

There is a potential drawback you need to be aware of if you use three people. The interviewee may feel dominated by all three bearing down at once. This does not generally worry very senior staff, but some managers are more relaxed and open with just an interviewer and note-taker.

Figure 5-5
Three on One

Group Interviews

Group interviews are when two or more interviewees are taken through an interview **as a group**. (Our record for a successful group interview is fifteen people.) Critical to the success of such a session is the maintenance of notes, during the course of the interview, which are **visible to everyone**. We have found that the use of process diagrams, information models and various other formal and informal graphic techniques, along with an overhead projector or flip charts, can act as a focal point for the group and can be used as the basis for questions to be asked and answers to be recorded, so that everyone in the session can keep pace, feel involved and contribute successfully, without frequent disagreement on terms and details. However, it should **not** be seen as an easy way of grouping a number of interviews into a short time, as a number of special skills in facilitation are needed to run this type of session successfully. (See Chapter 10 under "Feedback Sessions" for more details.)

**Figure 5-6
Eleven on Two!**

**Preparing
for an Interview**

Having concentrated on the logistics of setting up a series of interviews, let us now move on to the equally important task of preparing the content of the interviews.

Background Reading

Preparations for the interviews should begin as the interviews are being scheduled. Background reading helps to fill in the vocabulary of the organization; special terms are the first thing to look for. Annual reports, current reports on special topics, product literature and brochures are examples of the types of material we review. Other basic industry information comes from external sources and is of equal importance, as we need to look at an organization in the context of its industry. While we were at this stage on one project, there was an article in the *Financial Times* which cited the company and gave us not only an important external view but also a useful way to break the ice at the beginning of an interview. In the private sector we need to know who the leading businesses in that sector are, including their size and scale – what is the market share of the business we are working with? In the public sector it is helpful to identify the leading institutions, known for outstanding or good practices; for example, in the healthcare area, we may want to determine the leaders in hospital administration practice.

The objective of background reading is to identify important factors, both internal and external, about the business. Examples include:

- identifying major products or services
- knowing the organizational structure and identifying key personnel
- obtaining financial data relating to growth, market position, and other relevant aspects

- assessing general economic conditions for the industry
- identifying task-environment factors: key competitors, suppliers, etc.

Within the organization it is often easy to obtain the following types of information sources:

- annual report(s)
- organization charts
- product literature
- consultants' reports
- reports from task forces
- reports from steering committees
- current and previous business plans
- advertising brochures, and so on.

Industry and company information is available from external sources; for example, *Standard and Poor* in the United States, *Dun and Bradstreet* in the United Kingdom, *Dun's Europe* and, internationally, DIALOG and other online databases (see Appendix B). It is useful to obtain background information on:

- industry averages (see the Standard and Poor industry ratios)
- industry key issues
- industry indices
- market shares
- stock valuation
- market/competitor data for private enterprises.

For the public and 'non-profit' sector, background information may be obtained on leading institution 'models' and sector issues (e.g. healthcare/ administration), budget sources (from whom and what percentage). Journals of professional associations, reference libraries and the rapidly expanding online networks of information are all places to look for this type of information.

These are just a few baseline sets of information. You are seeking to be able to describe, in a few sentences, the basic business of the organization, its products and services and its relative (competitive) position in its own sector. The background material is filed for usage throughout the life of the project and should be made known and accessible to team members. It supplies basic information to focus the interviews and should stimulate questions to seek answers in the interviews. Comparative industry information is especially useful for eliciting detailed responses on the practicalities of a business situation.

During one interview, for example, Gordon Beam uses his knowledge of the travel industry when he asks: *"Will you be considering facilities for passengers to freshen up after a long flight without having to check into a hotel? Major airlines are now offering that service in some regions."*

In business analysis, you are looking for relevant information to create a complete picture. Too often, information-gathering effort focuses too narrowly on internal organizational information, at the sacrifice of a broader view of that organization in an industry and global context. Naturally, there must be some limit placed on information gathering, but the key is to obtain sufficient background to be able to probe sensibly how the organization operates and, particularly, what the main factors are that drive it. This requires some basic knowledge beyond the internal boundaries of the organization itself. Reports and other text materials are just one type of resource. Industry briefings by experienced people are another useful source of background information. Plan to establish time to talk to people (inside or outside the organization) who can provide information on some or all of the basics of the industry.

Interview Checklists

When we have built up a general picture, we apply that information to the task of drawing up lists that will be used to guide our questioning during the interviews. These lists can be of several kinds: general information lists (such as business objectives, to be asked about in all or most interviews) and topical lists for specialized information (such as financial issues) from specific interviewees.

Using checklists is a technique that helps to structure interviews without the inflexibility that a list of structured questions creates. Skilled interviewers do not rely on preworded questions, which tend to distract everyone from a natural flow of topics. A checklist provides a guide to the key topics that need to be covered; although the topics and their sequence will vary between interviews, the order of the items on each checklist is not significant – all that is necessary is that each item is covered at some point. For Atlantis Island Flights, the general checklist might include:

- ☐ Personnel
- ☐ Business objectives
- ☐ Travel volume and types expected
- ☐ Community/business relations
- ☐ Architectural style
- ☐ Size of hotel (number of rooms, facilities, etc.)
- ☐ Services to provide
- ☐ Financial implications.

These general checklists are used throughout all the interviews and provide a good cross-reference of opinion to similar topics within the organization. For instance, what do different interviewees cite as the business objectives for the organization? They also allow the interviewer to pose questions naturally by framing them in words to fit the flow of the interview. This, in turn, increases the building of rapport and mutual trust and leads to more candid replies. (See Appendix D for "Strategic Information Types".)

Within a specific functional area or business process, more detailed questions need to be asked. A personnel checklist, for example, might include:

☐ Job description

☐ Pension

☐ Recruiting

☐ Advertising

☐ Union

☐ Payroll

☐ Training

☐ Benefits.

You may think that experienced interviewers will not need basic checklists. They are always useful, though, as a guide and completeness check. When there are several people involved in the interviews, such as the note-taker and other team members, it becomes important to create checklists to ensure similar coverage in all interviews.

The major advantage of checklists is that they allow freedom for the interviewer to pose questions naturally to fit the situation, in contrast to preworded questions created before the interview. The result of prewritten questions is that they sound unnatural, formal, even amateur or insecure. A natural flow of conversation is what you are working to achieve.

On the practical side, you may find it useful to use a word processor to create the checklists, as they can then be easily modified for other interviews. In this manner, there is automatic project documentation for all of the interview checklists. At a later stage, a brief review will allow further interviews to be guided by past checklists when new information is required. Full documentation helps to eliminate redundancy in interview questions from one set of interviews to another. It is not uncommon in some organizations for people to resist further interviews on the grounds that they have already been interviewed (often by another project group). Whenever possible, documentation should build on information gained from previous interviews.

Interviewee Profiles

Taking the time and effort to familiarize yourself with the personal details of an interviewee is a courtesy. It is equally important to know how the individual fits into the organization, how long a job role has been held, and similar factors.

For the interview profiles, Gordon Brown and his team determine the following for each interviewee:

- full name and preferred form of address (e.g. Mr Singer, Ed, etc.)
- role in the organization and length of time in that role
- topics or business areas of expertise
- rapport items (hobbies, topical events, etc.) for 'ice-breakers'.

The interviewee profile enables you to:

- establish better rapport
- guide the interview, and therefore
- obtain more pertinent information.

Knowing the interviewee's background helps you to understand potential answers and to find the areas for which the interviewee is likely to have key answers. It means knowing common areas for ice-breakers – the sort of questions and remarks that can relax people and get the conservation going at the beginning of the interview. And, just as importantly, it means knowing of potentially sensitive areas to avoid or to approach carefully in an initial interview. You are preparing to look briefly at the world from the interviewee's perspective. That cannot be done armed only with a name and job title!

Preparing Materials

The following equipment, which needs to be organized in advance, can be used to support interviewing activities:

- Hardback notebooks – guaranteed to stay in chronological order and all in one piece!

- Whiteboards – useful for posting team information, scheduling, follow-up activities, etc. (whiteboards that photocopy are especially efficient).

- Wall charts or flip-chart paper – for creating a master schedule on the wall, showing master follow-up lists or communicating general information in the project room.

- Tape recorder – ideally taking ninety-minute tapes as it becomes a distraction, rather than an unobtrusive tool, if there is too much tape switching. Buy more tapes than you think you will need to avoid potential panic and a spare set of batteries also makes sense. The tape recorder should be tried and tested beforehand.

- Filing system – to hold notes and documents/materials obtained during the interviews. It is also of use during the feedback session.

- Computer – especially important during the consolidation of the notes and business modelling; that is, highlighting and summarizing information into lists, reports, diagrams and models. While word-processing files can support some of the consolidation activities, CASE tools are often used for project documentation and modelling. Multi-user CASE tools provide a data dictionary that supports complex projects and helps cross-check for accuracy and completeness amongst a number of team members.

Summary Checklist

☐ Interview roles assigned

☐ Briefing letter sent

☐ Interview scheduled and confirmed at briefing meeting

☐ Background reading

☐ Note-taking materials and other equipment available

☐ General interview checklist

☐ Topical interview checklist

☐ Interviewee profile.

Mind Set

This is your final task before each interview begins:

- Review the profile information and topical checklists.

- Identify the objectives of the interview and the special issues in that business area.

- Rehearse possible questions and anticipate answers. Develop additional questions that may be needed.

- Confirm each interview in advance.

Chapter

6

CONDUCTING A BUSINESS INTERVIEW

Introduction

Preparing for and conducting an interview is rather like performing in a play, with you as one of the main actors. At this stage in the theatrical process, you have been through rehearsals and are now ready for your first live performance. And in the interviewing process, you have completed the preparations behind the scenes: you have set objectives for the session, drawn up a checklist, prepared a profile of the interviewee and confirmed the appointment for the interview. After reviewing your preparations, you are ready to perform your role as an interviewer or note-taker on the interview team for the live interview.

Figure 6-1
The Stage is Set

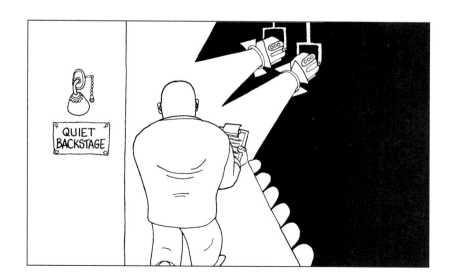

In this chapter we follow the action of one example scene (session) in a 'live interview'. Visualize the scene:

- the cast of characters
  - the interviewer
  - the note-taker
  - the interviewee (a marketing director)
  - the interviewee's secretary

- the setting
  - the office of the marketing director

- costumes
  - professional dress for the interview team (no jeans and T-shirts!)

- lighting
  - indirect (this is not an interrogation)

- sound effects
  - hopefully none (the secretary holds telephone calls and visitors)

- props
  - clock
  - coffee and refreshments
  - comfortable chairs and low table
  - tape recorder
  - notebooks
  - checklists.

We are now ready to begin the live interview.

SCENE I

The interviewing team comprises Jill Graham and Gordon Beam. Ed Singer, the Sales and Marketing Director, obviously knows Jill well and has already met Gordon on the site visit and at the briefing session. As Jill enters Ed's office, she extends her hand in greeting and tells him that she will be the interviewer and Gordon will be taking notes today. Jill knows that Ed is a keen yachtsman, and looking around the office she sees a model and photographs of his latest boat. These provide a point of interest for informal conversation before they begin the interview proper.

Ed motions to the interview team to take seats around a table. Jill selects a chair close to Ed and asks if they can control the bright sunlight shining into their eyes from a window behind the table. She explains that they have a long session scheduled and need to be comfortable. When Ed's secretary brings in coffee, he reminds her that there are to be no interruptions from calls or visitors during the interview.

Figure 6-2
The Seating Arrangements

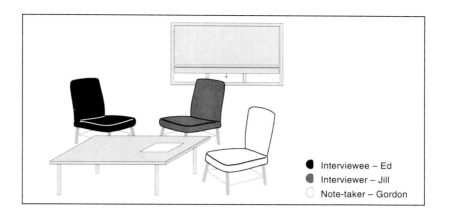

Interviewee – Ed
Interviewer – Jill
Note-taker – Gordon

To begin the session, Jill reviews where they are in the project and how the interview fits into the overall tasks to be done, referring back to the briefing session that all interviewees attended. She explains that the interview notes will be used for developing models of the business and describing the business requirements that will be shown during feedback sessions. Ed says that he understands the purpose of the interview and is glad to have the opportunity to talk to them at this early stage.

Gordon places the tape recorder on the table and asks permission to record the session. He stresses that the tapes will be confidential but the recorder can be turned off if there is any part of the discussion that Ed does not want on tape.

**Figure 6-3
Using the Tape Recorder**

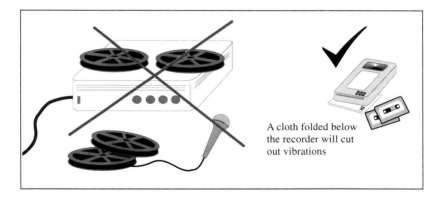

A cloth folded below the recorder will cut out vibrations

Jill now clearly sets the direction for the session. She outlines the need for strategic-level discussion and states that the focus will be on business issues, not on specific details of how things will be implemented. At this point, Ed relaxes and smiles, as he has been worried that Jill and Gordon would ask detailed questions for which he does not have answers.

The Open Questions

Jill starts by asking a few general, open questions:

"What are the main objectives for your first year in this new business?"

"What type of customers, or market, are you focusing on?"

"What market information have you used to help you determine your target market?"

Ed's responses lead naturally to other questions and Jill and Gordon refer to the checklist they prepared for this session.

Figure 6-4
Checklist for the Interview

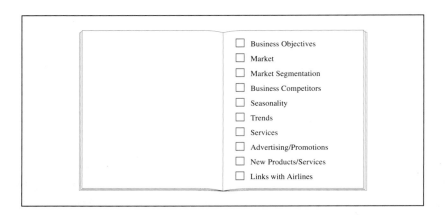

The checklist serves as a basis for developing questions, but Jill does not ask questions in any predefined order. The interview pace is natural, like a conversation. Jill controls the direction of the interview, however, and does not allow it to wander aimlessly or get diverted into side discussions that are irrelevant. At one point, Ed starts to digress into problems he had with a former boss. Jill listens, but senses that the information is not going to be relevant to this project, so she intervenes with a glance at her watch and a polite comment: *"Ed, we know your time is limited today, so could we return to what you were saying about the types of customers you are targeting. How do you expect these target markets to change in the future?"*

Jill carefully observes Ed's reactions to questions, responding to his non-verbal signals as well. When the interview begins, she notices that Ed looks slightly apprehensive, with his arms folded in a 'wait and see' manner. She uses this signal as a warning to proceed carefully and not to jump into any controversial topics too soon. She waits until Ed's non-verbal responses reflect acceptance and openness, with Ed now sitting in a relaxed manner, smiling during his replies. Jill encourages this change with good eye contact, returns Ed's smile and uses a positive, pleasing tone when she asks a question.

At one point, Ed asks if his reply to a question can be 'off the record' because he feels that some of the information about problems with the local planning authority is confidential. Gordon quickly turns off the tape recorder and stops taking notes on this point. When Ed completes the confidential reply he indicates to Gordon to continue with the recording.

The interview is scheduled for three hours. After one hour, Jill suggests a five-minute break: she wants to change the tapes without interrupting the flow of conversation. Jill uses the time to review the checklist to see what areas need to be addressed in the next part of the session. Ed is relieved: he still smokes occasionally and feels in need of a cigarette!

Aside

As you will appreciate, this interview is a good test of Jill's interpersonal skills. She is, after all, interviewing a colleague. No interviewer wants to have a bad interview, but in Jill's case she has to work with this person afterwards so it is especially important to be successful.

Jill is ultimately responsible for the success of the whole project and she was very keen to do some of the interviewing herself. Earlier, when they were scheduling the interviews, she and Gordon decided that this was a good one for Jill to lead as she and Ed tend to agree on the future direction of the company. You may remember that Gordon is to conduct the potentially difficult interview with Pete Stirling, the Finance Director.

SCENE II
Probing

The secretary uses the break as a time to offer extra refreshments. She brings bottled water and cups, as well as fresh coffee.

Jill is pleased with the interview so far. They are getting good infor-mation, much of it new to them. Before the interview, she was warned that Ed had complained that his time was valuable, and he could not spare three hours with so many deadlines to meet. Jill's questions, however, allow him to discuss issues that are very important to him and the probing of some of his answers has actually given him new ideas. For example, Jill asks what the differences are between business and holiday travellers in terms of services. As Ed outlines the types of services that are planned, Jill asks if they have considered offering several services that she has encountered as a business traveller – such as a combined telephone/fax/message machine in her room and a twenty-four-hour service for pressing clothes. Ed is interested as he has not considered these two services. This interchange of ideas gives him a good reason to continue the interview with genuine interest.

The atmosphere is relaxed as the session continues. Jill asks many questions relating to marketing issues: sources of market information, pricing issues, competitors, suppliers, services, evaluation of services, customer profiles, niche marketing, schedules, deadlines, promotions, travel offers and advertising. She is seeking a customer-oriented view and follows the business process from initially seeking a customer, then serving that customer, through to follow-up with the customer. Such a process view helps her to understand how the activities that Ed describes fit together. This will help later to build models that can be used to analyze where and how the company adds value for its customers, and is useful during the interview to provide a check on completeness. With the mental picture she has now built up of the marketing activities, Jill can identify any gaps in her knowledge.

Verbal Clues

The words you use to phrase your questions can act as verbal clues; different types of words will elicit different types of responses.

"Show Me"

Jill employs a range of questioning techniques during the session, including asking for ideas to be shown in a sketch to illustrate relationships or flow. When Ed tells her that they will be working closely with the airline side of the business to offer services, she asks him to show her the departments that will be working together from both sides of the organization. The verbal clue of 'show' is instantly picked up and Ed walks to a flip chart in his office to draw a quick diagram of these departments. It is a rough sketch but Gordon copies it carefully.

Figure 6-5
Pictures Are a Good Way to Record how Things Interrelate

Continuing this line of questioning, Jill next asks if Ed can show where suppliers fit into the picture. With a few more lines, Ed shows other parts of the company and how they fit into the emerging picture of relationships with external organizations. Jill uses words rich in visual representation in order to 'draw out' sketches and diagrams in a graphic response.

"Tell Me"

In contrast, Jill can use vocabulary that is more auditory and sound oriented, such as *"Tell me"* or *"What do you have to say about ...?"* to generate a spoken response. This is useful when precise descriptions are most easily conveyed by words and it is the type of response needed. For instance, if she asks, *"Tell me how many passengers you would expect at peak times"*, she will elicit a spoken reply.

"How do you feel?"

Finally, in questions that probe for an emotional response, Jill uses vocabulary such as *"How do you feel about ...?"* or *"What are your impressions of ...?"* The wording of such questions prompts a more subjective response. In some circumstances that is the type of information that is appropriate and required; on the other hand, it could be too general in other situations. By varying the type of question, Jill can vary the type of response and investigate a topic fully from many angles. Chapter 9 provides more detail on when and how to use verbal clues effectively.

Closed Questions

Jill asks many open questions that lead to full answers, but every so often she asks closed questions like *"How many?"* or *"When does that happen?"*

To obtain details, she probes with, *"Can you give me an example?"* She often asks for a specific example to clarify a more general question. When Ed tells her that they are interested in niche markets, she asks for an example and is given several, such as specialized markets for residential conferences and reunions. Jill is especially interested in these examples as she naturally wonders if there could be a possible conflict between different types of customer and the services they require. As she questions Ed on this point, she receives a more detailed description of the proposed services than they have heard about earlier. Gordon is kept very busy writing all the services that Ed proposes.

Opposites

Asking for opposites is a useful questioning technique. At one point Ed comments: *"Given our climate, the best season for us is spring."* Jill asks about the expected occupancy rate during their best season, which is a closed question. Then she asks for the opposite situation: *"What is the worst season for you?"* and follows this with: *"What do you expect your occupancy rate to be at that time?"*

Investigating contrasting situations helps to obtain a full, balanced picture of the business.

Critical Cases and Exceptions

Another technique Jill employs is sometimes called exceptions or 'critical cases'. She asks Ed to tell her of unusual cases or major incidents involving an area they are discussing. Jill has two objectives to seeking out these cases – in the process of exploring the exceptional she learns about the normal as well as unusual cases that the final system will have to cope with.

Ed tells her about a problem that arose at a conference dinner at another hotel. Several of the guests had special dietary requirements that the hotel was only able to meet with a major effort. Ed's description of the event provides Jill with extra questions. She asks for more details regarding the catering and conference arrangements to be offered by the new Atlantis Island Flights hotel.

Clarification

Occasionally Gordon interjects a question. As he makes his notes, he marks areas that require clarification. Then, at an appropriate time, he says: *"I'd like to go back to something we were discussing earlier – what did you mean, Ed, when you said ...?"* The timing of such questions needs to be natural, and Gordon waits until Jill pauses after completing a topic. As an experienced analyst and interviewer himself, he is particularly good at providing the support aspects of the note-taker's role. Once or twice, for example, when Ed's reply suggests he misunderstood the original question, Gordon intervenes, apparently seeking clarification, and asks a rephrased version of the original question.

Questions that are seeking clarification need to be asked with an open mind. Jill is careful to avoid leading questions or slanting them so that the answer is implied. Rather than asking Ed a question such as, *"Occupancy rates are usually lower in the autumn, aren't they?"*, she phrases it as, *"At what times of the year are the occupancy rates usually lower?"* The first question begs a 'yes' answer without necessarily exploring any other alternatives, whereas the second question is open and provides the opportunity for many different replies.

Confirmation

Jill uses confirming techniques to insure that she is not making incorrect assumptions (a trap she could easily fall into unless she is aware of the risk as she knows the company so well). From time to time during the interview, she briefly summarizes her understanding of a topic area and asks for confirmation. After a lengthy discussion of the niche markets, she begins the rephrasing: *"Ed, from what you have said so far, I understand that ..."*. She then waits for Ed either to show agreement or discuss any differences.

SCENE III

About thirty minutes before the scheduled time for an interview to end, there is a shift in the phase of the interview to move towards a successful conclusion.

Wrap-up

Jill starts the transition by summarizing the general topics covered so far and then asking: *"Is there anything that you had planned to discuss with us that we have not yet covered?"* Ed is especially pleased with this question as it provides him with a chance to cover several points that he had jotted down before the meeting. He starts out with what he states is his most immediately pressing problem – co-ordinating deadlines for promoting the new hotel and scheduling the activities for its opening. He elaborates on the issue and provides details on topics that are completely new to Jill, who eagerly follows up with more questions on the promotions for the opening.

As the final ten minutes approach, Gordon asks if there are any other people Ed thinks they should interview, either in this phase of the project or later. Ed suggests they interview one of his marketing staff for more detailed information on their proposed market research requirements. The contact information is noted by Gordon in a section for follow-up actions. At this point in the interview, Gordon also reminds Ed of the marketing brochures that he wants them to review. Ed provides directions to the office where Gordon can obtain them.

There are a few other follow-up actions that Gordon organizes. Then Jill reminds Ed of the planned feedback session where the findings and business models for the project will be discussed and confirmed with all the interviewees. The feedback session (scheduled six weeks in advance) will be held off site for a full day and Ed confirms the date and his availability.

The interview ends with genuine thank yous. Ed thanks them for the insights that came from several of Jill's comments. Jill and Gordon thank Ed for the time he has given them from a busy schedule.

Critique

The live interview is a success! In our review we can identify some key factors which led to its success.

The First Ten Minutes

The potential for a successful interview is established in the first ten minutes. The interviewer, Jill:

- 'breaks the ice' with an informal discussion about sailing
- establishes the purpose of the interview
- sets a comfortable pace
- observes non-verbal responses.

During the preliminaries of the interview, she determines if the interviewee attended a management briefing session. She reviews the purpose of the project and the type of information she is seeking with this interviewee. She begins the interview gradually (inexperienced interviewers sometimes ask in-depth questions too abruptly), setting a pace that is comfortable for herself and the interviewee. Jill maintains good eye contact and also observes her interviewee's non-verbal replies.

Questioning Techniques

The range of questioning techniques Jill (and Gordon) used during the interview is summarized below. You might like to review the description of the 'live interview' to see how she uses each of the following techniques and types of question. Can you identify examples in the interview?

☐ Checklist

A guide created during the planning session before the interview: it contains key words and key topics for obtaining information.

☐ Open Question

A type of question that requires a full reply to satisfy it, rather than a simple one or two word answer; for example, *"What are the main objectives for your first year in this new business?"*

☐ Closed Question

A type of question that may be answered with a 'yes', 'no' or simple factual reply; for example, *"When does that happen?"*

☐ Probing

Questions created to follow up and build on replies to previous questions; usually spontaneous, not part of a planned checklist. A good technique for maintaining continuity of dialogue during an interview.

☐ Clarification

Questions to focus on an area and seek clear understanding of information given. Summarizing and closed questions are often used, but avoid asking leading questions – you may seek confirmation of an erroneous view.

☐ Confirmation

Replaying current understanding by summarizing and asking for confirmation.

☐ Opposites

Information gathering by seeking the opposite or contrast to a reply. For example, following a discussion of the best season for occupancy rates, Jill asks, *"What is the worst season for you?"*

☐ Exceptions

Information gathering by exploring exceptions or critical incidents to help understand a specific area of the business.

☐ *"Show me"*

Encouraging graphic replies such as diagrams or sketches by using visual-oriented words in the question; for example, *"Could you show me what you mean ...?"* It may also involve using real models of products or other types of models.

☐ *"Tell me"*	Encouraging verbal details by using audio-oriented words to ask the question; for example, *"Tell me ..."*.
☐ *"How do you feel about...?"*	Encouraging subjective, intuitive opinions by using words related to emotion or feeling in framing the question.
☐ Wrap-up	Concluding questions that signal the final part of the session and allow sufficient time for the wrap-up; for example, *"Is there anything else you would like to tell us about?"* and *"Who else should we talk to, and why?"*

Active Listening

Jill is an active listener: she creates questions from the answers she receives. There is more though. The goal for a successful interview is for each person involved to be satisfied that the details explored have created a mutual understanding of the topic. For the interviewer, that requires putting aside personal assumptions and recognizing the assumptions that may cloud understanding. For the interviewee, it means responding openly; sometimes asking questions in return to explore fully the purpose of the question asked by the interviewer. No one is passive in a good session.

In the live interview, Jill uses confirming and probing techniques to help her go beyond her own knowledge and avoid false assumptions. Using confirming questions, she verifies that her understanding of Ed's answers matches what Ed intended.

Problem Handling

Jill handles the interview well and Ed is not difficult to interview. You may be unlucky, however, and suffer a different experience with an interview. The next few pages describe some common problems, which are listed below, and techniques that can help you solve them:

- the interviewee is defensive
- the interviewee is distracted
- the interviewee is incompatible with the interviewer
- too many questions are directed rapidly at the interviewee
- the interviewee controls the interview
- the interviewee uses preplanned answers
- the interviewee is a non-stop talker
- there are too many interruptions
- the interviewer talks too much
- the pace of the responses is slow
- the interviewee treats the interviewers in an unprofessional manner.

The Interviewee Is Defensive

Symptoms:

- the interviewee sits in a closed position with arms folded tightly
- the replies are short and do not give sufficient information.

Solution:

- probe carefully to determine the cause of the defensiveness
- show clearly how the answers will be used for the project and that the individual's performance is not an issue. A person who lacks confidence about the area being explored can become defensive
- seek areas of expertise to help relax the interviewee
- if the interviewee does not respond to these techniques, then address the issue directly. Say: *"We don't seem to be getting the information we need – is there anything wrong? Is there anything we can do to make it easier for you?"*

Example: the First Interview on a Small Strategy Study

Scenario

The interview of a senior manager in an educational institution starts with the normal process of introductions, reminding the interviewee why we are here, and we kick off with an open question: *"Take me through the life cycle of this educational establishment for a full year."*

In fact what happens is that we ask one question and the answer to a different question comes back! The answers we get are the sort of political answers that you would probably give to the main governing body of the institution – precise, accurate, careful answers. The interviewee is not relaxed; she is unsure of our situation and is protecting herself to a certain extent. This carries on for about forty-five minutes, by which time we have exhausted all our open questions because we are just not getting constructive answers to them. We are getting some useful, long-distance statements of direction and policy, but not useful information about what actually goes on in the institution from day to day.

To break through this particular situation and to relax the interviewee, the interviewer stands up, gets something out of his coat pocket and says: *"Oh, by the way, one of the things that we do with the information you tell us about in these interviews is to turn it into diagrams. I thought you might be interested. Would you like me to demonstrate one of these for you? It will only take a couple of minutes, and it will be a break from the interview."* He takes one of the subjects that was mentioned earlier in the interview and shows how a structured diagram can be built up representing the business objects that the interviewee has talked about. The interviewee gets very interested in this and reacts positively, asking questions as the model is developed. After a few minutes the interviewer sits down and returns to exactly the same question he started with an hour earlier. The interviewee is forthcoming with lots of useful information and extends the interview to make up for the lost time.

Technique By illustrating what will happen to the notes from the interview, the interviewee perceives no threat to her position (as she had done previously) and is, therefore, more forthcoming.

The Interviewee Is Distracted

Symptoms:

- urgent messages from secretary
- interviewee drums fingers on the table or taps foot impatiently
- reads through memos or other papers while responding to questions.

Solution:

- suggest that it may be better to reschedule the interview to allow the interviewee time to address the current urgent business
- discuss urgent areas of concern first.

Example: Interviewing the Manager in Charge of Quality Assurance

Scenario We have already done several interviews and prepared for this one very carefully. We have worked out a series of standard checklist questions, a series of open questions and a series of specific questions that have occurred to us from previous interviews that we need clarification on. We walk into the interview at 9.00 a.m. (having rechecked with his secretary the day before) to find that he looks very worried. His first words to us are, *"Thank goodness you're here"*, at which point we ask, *"Why? What's the problem?"* He replies, *"I've had a terrible week; in fact, I've had a terrible three weeks since I last saw you at the briefing session."*

So, we close our books and say, *"Tell us about it"*. What has happened is that a major problem has arisen on a site on installation. A fault that would normally occur perhaps once a year has been occurring ten times a week, and the fault is occurring on parts that his quality assurance people have been checking out. He is therefore held responsible and obviously this is a major issue. He tells us all the things that have been going on in the past three weeks – trips here, there and everywhere, discussions with his team leaders and people on site, and so on. After about ten minutes of just generally getting it 'off his chest', we open our books again and say: *"Take us through this from the very beginning, right back to the inception of the parts, how they were specified, designed, built. Who manufactured them. What was their quality assurance check and so on. Just bring us through the life cycle of one of those parts involved in the failure."*

Quite a long, relatively open question and it is the **only** question we ask. We do the whole interview from it because during the next three hours he tells us about the specification process, the design process, the entire life cycle of a generic part. When we do not understand something we probe a little and go into some depth. By the end of this time, several things have happened. The interviewee has been able to review the entire problem area from an objective outsider's point of view where there is no personal interest. He has looked at it from a global viewpoint – he is not talking to someone about a particular area – he is talking about the whole process. In doing so he manages to think of several things that might have caused the problem in the first place and several ways of solving it in the long term. So he gains value and, of course, from our perspective, we see probably three-quarters of the entire business from the single line of query.

Technique
: Be flexible in the interview and prepared to throw away all your preparation. Think on your feet and turn anything to your advantage.

The Interviewee Is Incompatible with the Interviewer

Symptoms:

- interviewee sits stiffly and does not respond in a relaxed manner
- glances with some hostility at the interviewer
- offers terse or unhelpful answers
- does not volunteer information.

Solution:

- reverse team roles so that the note-taker asks more questions; if this is better received continue with exchanged roles. If there is no change, try the techniques suggested for a defensive interviewee.

Too Many Questions Are Directed Rapidly at the Interviewee

Symptoms:

- note-taker and interviewer both talking
- the interviewee is interrupted during his answers
- the interviewee is sitting back.

Solution:

- improve teamwork, the interviewer should ask ninety-five per cent of the questions
- if the note-taker needs to intervene there should be a reversal of roles to keep the correct balance (see problem of incompatibility).

The Interviewee Controls the Interview

Symptoms:

- the interviewee starts to ask questions
- the interviewer or note-taker ends up talking more than the interviewee.

Solution:

- regain control by redirecting the type of questions, perhaps to a completely new area.

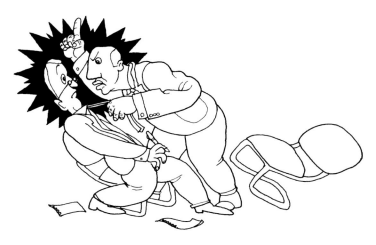

The Interviewee Uses Preplanned Answers

Symptoms:

- interviewee has preplanned answers
- interviewee continuously steers the interview to irrelevant topics.

Solution:

- allow the interviewee time to express what he thinks is important
- steer the interview to relevant areas
- look for opportunities to change the nature of the interview completely; for example, suggest a visit to a site to observe the topic that is being discussed.

Example: Detailed Interview with an Engineering Manager

Scenario   We are several interviews into a strategic business study. This is an interview with a senior engineer, the second of the type. He is a deputy manager in fact, and we have already interviewed one deputy manager from another similar, but different, engineering background. The intention of the interview is to make sure we have not missed anything in detail;

and to satisfy the sponsor that we have covered the ground, because quite often, as in this case, the two positions held by the deputy managers are perceived as being in totally different businesses. They might have been very different, but in reality they turn out to be very similar.

We arrive armed with a whole series of questions, such as, *"What do you do? Take me through a typical day. What happens in the event of a major failure – what would you do to recover the situation?"*, and a series of checklist questions based on reading around the subject. During the early part of the interview, we ask several open questions about what he does and in each case he says, *"Before I answer that I must tell you about ..."*, and he tells us about a subject that is heavily to do with the engineering aspects, the stresses and structures, the types of material used, and so on. We try another open question and he answers coherently about that area, but not in sufficient detail to be of any use. He does, however, go into the safety aspects, different degrees or zones for safety, security mechanisms, protection mechanisms, and so on. After an hour and a half we have still not managed to get answers to any of our questions. We **have** learned a tremendous amount about the engineering, the safety and all those aspects of his work (it is really rather interesting!). Then he actually pulls out the checklist he has been running through in his mind. It turns out in subsequent discussions that the night before the interview he spent three hours working out what he thought we were interested in and decided to tell us all about the mechanisms used to run the plant. This is extremely good background material and we use it subsequently for examples in the feedback session to bring to life the business objectives and the various models of the business (entity relationship diagrams, function models, etc.). We are very impressed with the note-taker who manages to take copious notes throughout. However, reviewing the notes later, we decide they are mostly irrelevant. Other than as examples, there is no meat in them at all.

At the end of this period, the interviewer says: *"Thank you for a most interesting afternoon. By the way, if you've got time, is there any chance of you taking us around the plant and just showing us the sort of things you've been talking about?"* The engineer readily agrees and relaxes now that he is out of the interview situation. We walk around the plant – up and down ladders, along corridors, everywhere. Wherever we see anything happening, we ask, *"What do they do?"* and he tells us. Or we ask, *"What is that information there for? What does that sign mean?"* In other words, as we travel round we ask open questions about what is being done or what something is used for, and in the process we take very detailed interview notes. Quite difficult at times, climbing up a ladder, walking along a gantry, and so on. (We are even more impressed with the note-taker after this.) The analysis of this particular interview is done using the notes taken going round the plant, as opposed to earlier notes.

| Flexibility | Flexibility is often required. It is impossible to preplan for every detail of an interview. An interviewer needs to make the best use of a change in plans so knowing how to adapt is important. The use of an interesting case is not part of the original plan, but by recognizing the opportunity the interview team is very successful in obtaining information. |

The Interviewee Is a Non-stop Talker

Symptom:

- there are virtually no pauses within lengthy responses.

Solution:

- redirect through gentle interruptions by the interviewer
- make sure key areas are addressed early
- suggest making out a map of key areas to establish a menu of topics with the interviewee, then try to split time sensibly between topics. This allows you to interrupt with: *"That's interesting, but I think we should try to cover all the ground if possible – perhaps you could tell us about one of these other topics and we can come back to finish this discussion if we have time at the end."*

There Are Too Many Interruptions

Symptoms:

- the phone continually rings
- visitors come to the door.

Solution:

- try to prevent this by reminding the interviewee and whoever handles calls and visitors that the session should not be interrupted
- if calls are still interrupting the session, check on their urgency
- if necessary, reschedule the interview, as suggested in the problem of the distracted interviewee.

The Interviewer Talks Too Much

Symptoms:

- the interviewee sits quietly
- the interviewer is talking more than twenty per cent of the time.

Solution:

- the note-taker can act as a monitor and signal if the balance of discussion is moving towards the interviewer. The aim is for the interviewee to do about eighty per cent of the talking.

The Pace of the Responses Is Slow

Symptom:

- the interviewer consistently interrupts (unintentionally)
- the interviewer completes sentences for the interviewee.

Solution:

- minimize cross-talk (two people talking at the same time) by listening carefully to the pace of the interviewee's replies. A slower-spoken person can mislead a faster speaker, who may expect a faster pace in the reply.

The Interviewee Treats the Interviewers in an Unprofessional Manner

Symptom:

- interviewee is condescending in tone and manner.

Solution:

- establish the professional credentials of the team during the briefing session before the interview. Conduct the interview in a professional manner, with the appropriate level of formality
- this may be a problem especially in a work situation when the interviewer is in a junior role. Try to obtain team members who can work at ease at all levels. Dress professionally to provide a visual clue to the importance of the interview.

These are just some of the difficult situations that can occur during an interview. Prepare yourself for handling such problems by considering the possible solutions and planning what you might do if the problem occurs at an interview you are conducting.

Consolidation

The next step after conducting the interview is to consolidate the notes. In Chapter 8, we describe techniques to consolidate notes and materials from an interview. But first let us review how the notes were created.

Chapter

7

NOTE-TAKING

In this chapter we define the role of the note-taker, introduce a number of practical techniques for taking notes, and finish with some simple exercises for practising these techniques.

The Note-taker's Role

The three main tasks in an interview are:

- conducting the conversation
- intelligently analyzing the information as it is received and
- recording the information that the interviewee gives.

Each of these tasks is quite demanding on its own. To ask a single person to perform all three in a one-to-one interview is asking a great deal indeed. It is much better to have at least two people conducting the interview – an interviewer **and** a note-taker. The note-taker's primary responsibilities are to record information, to help the interviewer by analyzing this information as it is received, and to ask clarification and follow-up questions. The interviewer is then free to concentrate on the task of conducting the conversation.

There are other advantages to having two people present. If, for example, the person being interviewed and the interviewer have a clash of personalities, the note-taker and the interviewer can swap roles. Taking notes is not a passive process: the note-taker is analyzing while recording, and if the interviewee should stop talking or the interviewer run out of questions, the note-taker can provide an accurate set of follow-up questions. Scheduling to have two people present also provides back-up in case one of the interviewing team is unavoidably detained or ill on the day. The event itself can still go ahead, with the remaining team member conducting a one-to-one interview, although you will obviously lose the advantages of the team approach.

In international situations, local language may be a consideration – a note-taker who does not understand the language of the interviewee is not a lot of use! Of course, this also applies to the interviewer but not to the same extent. While it is possible to have a meaningful discussion through a competent translator, detail and nuances in the replies may be lost and conversation will flow less easily. Even where there is apparently no language barrier, there can be problems: a Parisian, an Algerian, a Vietnamese and an American may all say the same words in impeccable French, and they may all mean something slightly different because their use of words is shaped by their own cultures. Such language and cultural issues need to be confronted in the planning phase, when an interviewer and note-taker are being assigned. Choose a note-taker who shares the language skills of the interviewee to avoid the situation where the note-taker is recording material translated by an interpreter.

Skills

First and foremost, note-takers need to develop the skill of 'unfiltered' listening combined with the ability to record key concepts and details. You may notice an apparent contradiction here. If the listening is unfiltered, will the recording not be similarly all embracing?

Unfiltered Listening

By unfiltered listening we mean that the note-taker captures relevant words in the **exact** form used by the interviewee – not filtered, modified or summarized. For instance, if the interviewee uses the word customer the note-taker should record the word customer, not client or some other synonym. Certain terms may have a very exact meaning in a particular enterprise, so precision is important.

The words people choose often reveal their attitude to what they are describing, but they may also reflect their own personalities and cultures. The British, for example, have a tendency to use understatement. The person who says *"I'm not too bad at that"* may well be a whiz-kid at it, but it is culturally unacceptable to say so. Everyone in Britain understands the meaning behind the apparent modesty. In another case where words cannot always be taken at face value, different teachers may describe the same class of children variously as *'3C'*, *'my third-year Chemistry group'* or *'a pack of idiots'*. The teacher of the pack of idiots may truly dislike this class, but equally well may simply have had a tough lesson with them that day, or indeed may be fond of them, despite their faults. If you suspect that the words an interviewee uses should not be taken literally you can add annotations as you record them. By the end of the interview, you should understand the interviewee sufficiently to grasp the true meaning. Although we have stressed the importance of recording words exactly, it is not necessary to record **every** word – the emphasis here is on capturing the **relevant** words.

A novice note-taker, Steve, suffered dreadfully from writer's cramp after an interview. It transpired that he had attempted to write absolutely everything down, including each *'um'*, *'ah'* and *'I think'*. After the interview, he spent hours trying to read his handwriting, which had deteriorated as the interview progressed and, because he had been concentrating so hard on writing everything down, he had not really been listening to what was being said. Needless to say, although it was a very hard lesson, he has not made the same mistake since. Arguably, the more serious mistake was made by the interview planner. The role of note-taker should be performed by an experienced analyst, and no experienced analyst would make the elementary mistake of trying to take a verbatim copy of an interview and completely overlooking the task of intelligent analysis of the information being received.

Endurance

A second important aspect of successful note-taking is endurance. An interview can last for four hours or more, and to concentrate, record and periodically summarize notes for this length of time is extremely difficult. Do not imagine that all interviews are conducted in comfortable offices. Some of our best interviews have been conducted 'on the hoof'. The manager of a factory may find it much easier to take you on a conducted tour of the plant, explaining what is going on in a real context and allowing the interviewer to ask all sorts of questions about what is actually happening and what people are doing during the manufacturing process. But pity the poor note-taker, trying to hear all that is said above the din of the machinery, writing while walking around, trying to avoid tripping over obstacles or slipping on a catwalk. Circumstances like these make this role a real challenge!

Support the Interviewer

In addition to the listening and writing functions of a note-taker, there are important support tasks. Note-taker and interviewer are a team, and although the lion's share of the questioning is done by the interviewer, the occasional well-placed question from the note-taker can often help. In one case, the note-taker may ask for more details to a particular response; in another case, where the interviewee has not understood a question as it was originally asked, the note-taker can aid both the interviewer and interviewee by rephrasing it.

The role of the note-taker in asking questions and supporting the interviewer is discussed in Chapter 6. As he makes his notes, Gordon Beam marks areas that will need further clarification questions and asks some of the 'tidying up' questions at the end of the interview (see pages 78–9). Some other support tasks are examined in "Problem Handling" (page 84 et seq.).

Techniques

The intention is to record everything of relevance during an interview in a way that can be used later. Although the end result is the same, the method of achieving this depends upon the specific situation and the personal preferences of the note-taker. Here is a selection of simple note-taking techniques that can be used for recording information:

Scripts

Perhaps the most obvious way of taking notes is to make a verbatim record of the interview, either in longhand or shorthand. If you attempt this feat in longhand, like Steve the novice note-taker, you may suffer writer's cramp. If you have excellent shorthand skills, you will be able to meet the challenge, but unfortunately you will have to transcribe your notes before other people can use them. Unless you are producing reports of government or court proceedings or perhaps recording a police interview, it is most unlikely that you will need a verbatim record. An adequate attempt can usually be made by simply writing quickly and concentrating on getting down the **key points** and leaving out the 'ums', 'ahs' and other phrases that add little value in terms of information gained.

For example, during her interview Chris Hayley from Human Resources talks enthusiastically about an idea of hers:

> *"Well, I did have an idea last Tuesday, which I felt would help with the recruitment of staff for the new hotel. As we are going to need so many new members of staff, I thought it might be worth considering having an 'open day' at the end of the year, during which senior management could meet prospective employees and conduct preliminary interviews.*

I thought we could organize the day by arranging small tours around the complex – we could ask the secretaries if they would like to get involved. We can also have a word with catering, in due course, about making the necessary arrangements for coffee and lunch. Oh, and what do you think about getting Marketing involved as well, in case anyone has any really bright ideas on the day?"

The note-taker picks out key points and perhaps writes:

"hold open day – conduct preliminary interviews – tours – catering – Marketing (ideas)"

In other words, as a note-taker, you listen to a few sentences and note down the essence of what you hear, leaving out words that do not add any information in themselves. You may find these sample notes from Chris Hayley's interview rather cryptic. Certainly some useful points have been missed. What if consolidation is delayed and you feel you cannot rely too much on your memory? With experience you will learn where to strike a balance that works for you, not only in the amount of detail you need to record but between the different techniques for recording it.

When an interviewee who obviously understands a topic very well makes an assertion, it is worth recording this in quotes with the interviewee's initials after it. You can often detect an assertion by the way the words are delivered – in an emphatic tone, with authority, followed by a short pause to let it sink in. Repetition of such a statement stresses its importance to the speaker. Should you choose not to record this in some way, perhaps because you personally disagree with the assertion, the interviewee will see that you have not made special note of it and may keep returning to this point. You may get stuck on this topic for some time or, even worse, lose the confidence of your interviewee. Later on, after you have conducted a number of interviews for a project, you will be able to judge better which assertions are valid and should be retained for further use, including some you may have disagreed with at the time of the interviews.

If you use the script technique as your main or only form of taking notes, the importance of being able to consolidate your notes as soon as possible after the interview cannot be overstressed. The consolidation process, which is covered in the next chapter, relies on being able to re-establish your understanding of what the interviewee **meant** rather than what he or she **said** by looking at your notes.

You now need to consider how you will actually organize your notes. If you simply jot them down on a pad of paper you may miss out on analysis opportunities during the interview (or even lose parts of them when you separate the sheets later!). We generally use a hardback notebook, writing the notes on one side only, reserving the opposite page for consolidation.

Key points or issues noted during the interview can be picked out and noted on the consolidation pages.

The diagram below shows some of the notes taken during the interview with Chris Hayley. Any set of interview notes needs to start with the date and the names of the interviewee, interviewer and note-taker, and it is useful to repeat, at the very least, the date and the interviewee's name on each following page and tape. You may feel we are stating the obvious here, but it is surprising how many otherwise competent note-takers head for an interview with a blank notepad and emerge with scribbled notes on unlabelled loose pages. For full reference details, you might attach the interviewee's business card to the initial page.

Figure 7-1
Layout for a
Note-taker's Book

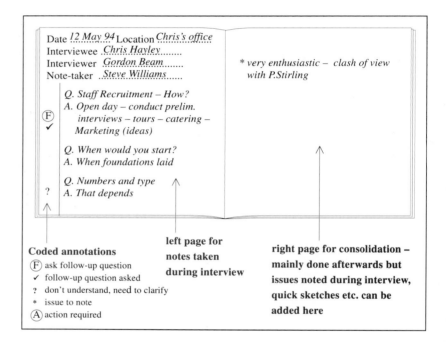

Date *12 May 94* Location *Chris's office*
Interviewee *Chris Hayley*
Interviewer *Gordon Beam*
Note-taker *Steve Williams*

(F) ✓
Q. Staff Recruitment – How?
A. Open day – conduct prelim.
* interviews – tours – catering –*
* Marketing (ideas)*

Q. When would you start?
A. When foundations laid

?
Q. Numbers and type
A. That depends

* *very enthusiastic – clash of view*
  with P.Stirling

Coded annotations
(F) ask follow-up question
✓ follow-up question asked
? don't understand, need to clarify
* issue to note
(A) action required

left page for notes taken during interview

right page for consolidation – mainly done afterwards but issues noted during interview, quick sketches etc. can be added here

Although many, perhaps most, note-takers cannot use shorthand, there is no reason why you should not invent your own code to annotate your notes or to save you writing the same thing again and again. In the example above the note-taker has added some simple annotations in the margin. Later in the interview or during consolidation he can easily scan his notes and pick out points he wants to check on. A tick (check mark) through the annotation will show that the follow-up has been made. Ideally an interviewer and note-taker will use an agreed code. Then, should they swap roles during the interview, they will be able to follow each other's notes (provided they can read each other's writing).

Tape Recording

Tape recording an interview is a very efficient way of recording exactly what is said (obviously!). Unfortunately, it is not so easy to use during consolidation, as we will discuss later, so we do not recommend it as a primary method of taking notes. We do, however, suggest using a tape recorder as a **back-up** method.

Do remember when arranging interviews to ask each person for permission to record what they say. It is also important to advise your interviewees that the tape recording can be stopped at any time should they so wish. An interviewee who may be willing to talk about sensitive issues 'off the record' may feel uncomfortable about committing statements to a tape recording. This is an unexpected bonus of using the tape as a back-up medium: it may reveal sensitive areas that might not otherwise have been obvious. The tape recorder can provide a barometer of sensitivity to issues, which helps to build a more realistic picture.

If you decide to make a tape recording, a common-sense checklist will help you to avoid some pitfalls to ensure that the taping does not interfere with the interview itself:

- check that the device works before you start the interview
- take spare batteries for the recording device
- have enough spare tapes for the expected duration of the interview, plus a couple extra in case the interview is extended
- organize your tapes in advance – number and label them with the date and names of people involved, as with written notes, and use them in sequence
- make a note of the time against your written notes every 15 minutes or so to act as a fast 'index' into the tape recording. You are also less likely to forget to put in new tapes when necessary if you are aware of the time.
- take something to set underneath the tape recorder or microphone to prevent noise from vibration affecting the recording – the person you are interviewing may start thumping the desk for emphasis! A small block of foam or a handkerchief works well.

Tapes are especially useful for recording rapid descriptions and details as a note-taker will find it difficult to capture all the information when someone is talking rapidly. However, a tape recording is no substitute for notes as it is so time-consuming to have to listen to a complete set of tapes again. Imagine having to sit through a full four-hour interview a second time! In practice, we have found this to be a lengthy and inefficient way of consolidating an interview compared with handwritten notes. The tape recording provides a useful back-up in cases where the written notes are incomplete or you feel there is some point that you need to examine very carefully. The sound recording will have picked up some subtle aspects such as the tone of the interview, nuances and possibly emotional attachment to certain topics which may be missed by using notes alone.

One final point; a tape recorder is also a useful way of reviewing and assessing (possibly even training) an interviewer. See how many of those questions really were open, spot the mistakes that were made so they do not become habits, and so on.

Formal Modelling during Note-taking

The ability to model as you take notes is a useful skill. An experienced note-taker who is also a competent modeller will often reserve a portion of the page to sketch models during the interview itself, perhaps part of a business process or an area of a business model showing the objects identified by the interview. This may reveal questions that need to be asked and lead to further relevant topics being discussed. The model may even be used with the interviewee in order to ask clarification questions.

Figure 7-2 Modelling during Note-taking

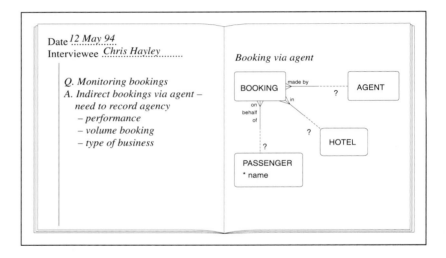

This method of note-taking is something to aim for rather than standard practice, as it requires a good deal of skill and experience.

Other Diagrams for Note-taking

Many people find it easier to grasp concepts that are presented in a visual form. As they say, *"a picture paints a thousand words"*. There is a great opportunity here for you to use your own visual shorthand. Using simple sketches or informal diagrams can enrich the meaning of your written notes and bring them to life when you return to them for consolidation. They can also be used to good effect during the interview to help you confirm or clarify something and to stimulate follow-up questions.

Cause and Effect Diagrams

If you are discussing a complex topic where many things are interlinked it can be difficult to identify and understand all the interactions when you restrict yourself to the spoken word, as this imaginary extract from an article in the financial pages of a newspaper indicates:

> *... A vicious circle can result from failure to cut public spending. As the tax burden on employers increases, they become less competitive and tend to employ fewer workers. This in turn increases the burden on public spending, requiring an increase of taxes on employers. The Chancellor's budget offers Britain an opportunity to reverse these effects, even though he has raised taxes to reduce borrowing so that interest costs can fall. If such a turn around in the supply side is achieved, the British government will ultimately be spending more in total (though less as a share of GDP), and there will be fewer people on whom it has to be spent ...*

You can construct a simple diagram to represent your understanding of how one aspect of this topic may lead to another. Essentially, it helps you to examine cause and effect, and consequences. Until you set out what you already know, or think you know, in a visual form you will probably not see all the consequences of a particular event. Figure 7-3 sets out our understanding of the interactions of the global economy. Presented like this it becomes much easier to spot missing or improbable interactions. For example, what effect will falling interest costs have? Will they improve competitiveness? Allow companies to employ more workers?

**Figure 7-3
Ad hoc Diagram to
Represent Economic
Interactions**

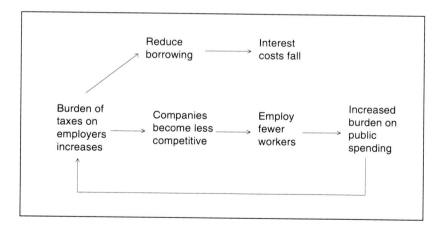

These diagrams can be used to test your understanding of a situation and act as an impartial tool for examining contentious points. If you try to feed back your understanding of a complex issue in words, as soon as you reach a contentious point your interviewee may interrupt and the discussion can get stuck at this point. With a diagram you have an opportunity to feed back the whole picture before you get bogged down. To ask an interviewee to confirm your understanding, you could try:

"Can I test my understanding of what you just said?" as you show a diagram to the interviewee. Pointing to each relevant part as you read round the diagram, *"I have written companies become less competitive, which may lead to them employing fewer workers, which may lead to an increased burden on public spending ..."*

The interviewee will often interrupt and help correct the diagram as this form of visual presentation of ideas is so easy to understand and use. Even if some parts are wrong you may get confirmation that it is essentially correct, allowing you to concentrate on resolving any disputed points.

Using Pictures

During an interview with a personnel manager you may collect a lot of information about the job roles of company employees and how many people are employed in each role. You could replay this in words – rather time-consuming, and quite a memory and concentration feat for your listener. A table would be better than words alone but the reader still needs time to compare the various entries. With a fully visual form like a bar graph or pie chart, the viewer can grasp the whole picture at a glance. It is second nature to most of us to present information with a numerical content in a structured visual way. But less structured information can also be presented in an interesting visual form. During the interview with the personnel manager you may be looking at staff turnover: how and why people join the company, why they leave it, and the sort of things in the workplace that have an impact on staff turnover. You can make a quick sketch of your understanding of this to discuss with your interviewee.

Figure 7-4
Using Pictures for a
Personnel Interview

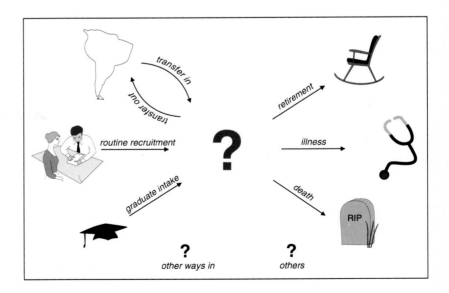

This can help you to focus on ill-defined areas, leading to follow-up questions. Figure 7-4 above shows one way of presenting this visually; notice the question mark in the centre showing an entire area that needs to be defined.

You will remember we said earlier that note-taking was a skilled job. The ideal so far is a good active listener; an excellent analyst; an experienced modeller; we want you to be able to switch roles at a moment's notice and take over as interviewer; and now we want you to be an artist? No, it is not necessary to be an artist to use pictures and diagrams effectively. After all, as small children we were all able to communicate using pictures before we learned to use a written language. 'Stick people' and rough outlines work fine in practice.

Figure 7-4 would still be useful with just the words presented in the diagrammatic form. It is up to you how you choose to do it; you can create ad hoc diagrams with or without pictures and with or without your own rules and conventions. Any sketches you make can be used later for analysis or transformed into a more structured form using a structured modelling technique. Figure 7-5 shows a Business Process Diagram for one way of getting a job with Atlantis Island Flights.

Figure 7-5
Structured Process Model

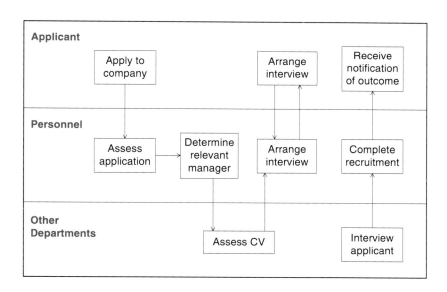

Mind Mapping

Some people like to organize their thoughts in a structured written form, perhaps like this book with headings and lists and bullet points, maybe with visual clues such as colour or underlining to emphasize key points. When you were at school or college, if you missed a lesson and had to borrow someone's notes these were the ideal people to approach.

Other people prefer a much more pictorial style and may derive their own individual diagrammatic methods. These may simply be a development of the spider-like diagrams used by school children, where a key point is written in the centre and things describing it are written on radiating legs. Or they be much more sophisticated methods that employ the brain's ability to recognize patterns and to create associations between things based on colours, shapes, proximity and similarity. Mind mapping is one such technique that can be employed to assist memory recall. It is useful both during an interview and afterwards for consolidation. While not recommended as a primary note-taking technique for long interviews, it can be used by an **interviewer** to take very brief notes. It also helps with completeness checking and can stimulate original thought and ideas, depending on when and how it is used.

An Example Mind Map

The mind map in Figure 7-6 might have been produced from part of an interview with Chris Hayley. We have highlighted the parts of the map that relate to the Open Day for recruitment discussed in an earlier section.

Figure 7-6
An Example Mind Map

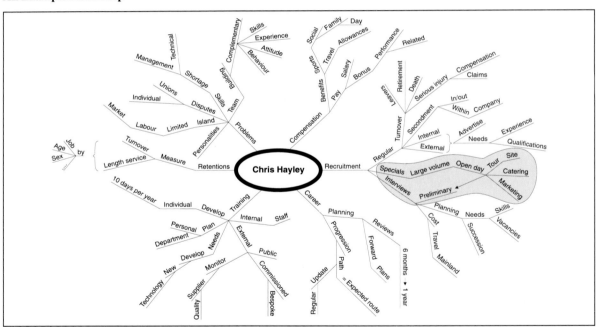

As you can see, a mind map is a tree of connections, starting in the middle of the page and radiating outwards, getting more specific as they go (a technique popularized by Buzan, 1974). It is essentially no more than a mechanism for committing a series of thoughts to paper. When applied in an interview situation, what the interviewee says creates a 'picture' in the mind of the note-taker – it is this picture that the note-taker transfers to the mind map by rapidly classifying key words and phrases.

People who enjoy using this technique often add their own modifications and employ it in many different situations. In a brainstorming session, for example, it can be used to add some structure to the process. You may decide to add icons or symbols to the diagram to indicate a similarity or a link between different branches or you may actually add lines and links between the outer branches. Mind maps tend to be very personal and a map that is an accurate *aide-mémoire* to the author may be interpreted in a completely different way by someone else. When a group of people want to use and share mind maps, these misinterpretation problems can be minimized by setting some guidelines:

- work out from the centre of the page
- expand to fill the space
- write on the line
- use only one word, or very short phrase, per line
- connect the lines in the relevant place
- work fast
- write whatever occurs to you – do not consciously filter out words
- start each new topic on a main branch.

Ideas and thoughts are often triggered by apparently unrelated words. Sometimes, puns on words, words that rhyme or quite the strangest things cause you to think of something. The trick with mind mapping is to get your mind to flow and not to resist it – do not stop to rationalize consciously while you are developing the map.

The mind map represents a summary of topics that have been covered and, to an extent, the way in which those topics are interrelated. This can help an interviewer to see where the interview has been so far and act continually as a reminder of key facts. This helps with phrasing related questions, such as:

> *"A while ago you mentioned the limited labour market on the islands being a problem for your business – how does what we've just been talking about affect your ability to recruit and retain new staff?"*

If you run dry or the interview slows down for any reason, reread and annotate your map to help you remember what the interviewee **meant**:

- clarify the map and add things from memory
- use colour; for example, code the most important things in red
- block, box in or otherwise enclose related areas of the map
- highlight or shade significant areas to make them stand out.

(You might do well to save some of this consolidation until after the interview in case it detracts from getting the interview flowing again.)

If you are using mind mapping as a preparation technique to note down something very important, such as a structure for the next interview, after you have constructed the map review it briefly every so often, looking at it for about a minute or less:

- ten minutes after its construction
- thirty minutes after its construction
- a few hours later and
- immediately before the interview.

This brief review acts as a very fast refresher, reinforcing the original picture in your mind. You will find with practice that you can recall almost all the detailed thoughts with just a few seconds of reading the map. Something that may surprise you initially is how long this will stay in your mind after the event; the accuracy with which it can be recalled weeks, months or even years later is staggering. Used in this way, a mind map can be a very effective way to maintain a structure for an interview, either by taking the map along to the interview or just holding the image in your mind!

Mind mapping rarely feels natural initially – practice really does make perfect. If you are going to try it as a note-taking technique, you might like to practise in the following situations:

- map this book as you read it
- map fifteen minutes of a news bulletin from television or radio
- map a plan for next year's holiday.

Summary

Whatever format for note-taking you select, and you will probably want to mix two or three preferred techniques, bear in mind that the notes are a record for information gathering purposes. This information will be required by the team as a whole. The simplest layout with a script of the key points is perfectly adequate and usually a good technique to start with.

The role of note-taker is not a passive one: it is active and can play a critical role in clarifying points of contention. As a minimum, a good note-taker obtains factual information, notes the tone of the interview and helps to form any questions arising during the interview. This second perspective during the interview can be invaluable. Points that may be clear to the interviewer may not provide sufficient information for another person, or the interviewee may not understand a question asked by the interviewer. In such situations the note-taker can probe an answer or restate a question for clarification.

Practical Exercise

A novice note-taker can find the pace of an interview challenging and the effort tiring. Developing skills always requires practice so that some aspects become more automatic. This then allows the practitioner to concentrate on developing further skills. Unfiltered listening and note-taking are two skills to practise, and a degree of endurance and concentration over long periods can be cultivated by practice sessions. Try the following opportunities to practise listening and note-taking skills:

- recordings of previous interviews
- meetings – volunteer to take the minutes
- television and radio newscasts and talk shows
- tape recordings
- lectures and presentations
- telephone conversations
- recorded books
- recorded speeches and, of course,
- actual interview practice.

Take the time to consciously practise the skills of a note-taker for an information-gathering interview. Set up the practice session for a minimum of half an hour to test your concentration. Try to avoid interruptions, just as you would during an actual interview.

Practice Session

You can create your own practice exercise using one of the situations suggested above:

- write down your objectives for the information gathering
- organize your notebook format
- set up a tape recorder
- concentrate
- conduct the exercise, taking notes as you go
- listen carefully
- take notes, using either the technique you find most natural or one that you want to practise
- draft follow-up questions during the practice session
- note tone, nuances and feelings projected beyond the words.

After the session, review your experience and evaluate the quality of the information you have captured. Are you satisfied that you have sufficient information in your selected topic area? If not, how can you improve next time? Do you have time for another practice session? (Now that you have half an hour of notes, save them for the practical exercise on consolidation in Chapter 8.)

If you have a tape or video recording of dialogue such as an interview on a news or current affairs programme, try running it a number of times, but take notes using a different technique each time.

Test your Skills

Answer the following multiple choice questions to see how you shape up as a note-taker.

1. You are starting an interview with a chief executive and need to record the event. Do you:

   a) Slip the recorder onto the table unobtrusively and quietly set it running.

   b) Wait until answers of some real substance emerge before introducing the recorder and checking there is sufficient tape and battery power, as the early conversation is quite general.

   c) Ask if it is all right to record the interview and assure the interviewee that the recording can be turned off in order to remain confidential.

2. The interviewer has asked a question that seems to confuse the interviewee and you think you can see why the confusion has arisen. Do you:

   a) Rephrase the question using a slightly different approach.

   b) Offer one potential answer to the question to 'start the interviewee off'.

   c) Do nothing and wait for the interviewer to try again.

3. The production director describes the use of a manufacturing method that you know has caused problems for another company. Do you:

   a) Note verbatim exactly what the interviewee says.

   b) Note the method and the fact that this causes the problems you suspect.

   c) Note the method and follow up with a question asking whether or not the problems you suspect are being experienced here.

4. You get lost in a particularly complex statement of how clients are dealt with. Do you:

   a) Try to think of a similar experience from your past in order to fill in your notes.

   b) Stop the interviewee and ask him to repeat parts of the explanation.

   c) Leave a gap in the notes and record the time so that this piece can be found on the tape recorder.

5. The interviewee says: *"After taking the order from a client we usually thoroughly check their credit status to see if their credit is OK and either reject the order or go ahead and process it."* Do you write:

   a) Client → take order → check credit → reject or process order

   b) Take customer order, check credit and reject or accept.

   c) Take order from client and check credit status thoroughly (see if credit is OK) then reject order or go ahead and process it.

Now turn over the page to check your rating on the answer grid.

Answer Grid for Test

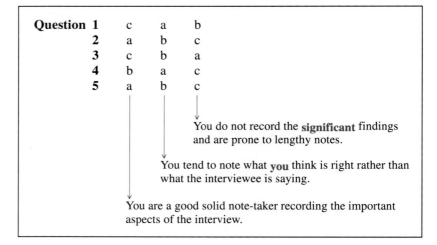

Question 1	c	a	b
2	a	b	c
3	c	b	a
4	b	a	c
5	a	b	c

You do not record the **significant** findings and are prone to lengthy notes.

You tend to note what **you** think is right rather than what the interviewee is saying.

You are a good solid note-taker recording the important aspects of the interview.

Chapter

8 USING THE INTERVIEW MATERIAL

Introduction

We made it! After all the careful planning and preparation, the interview took place. Now both interviewer and note-taker find themselves with:

- about forty pages of notes
- four ninety-minute tapes
- some understanding of the subject matter, but a great deal of irrelevant material in mind, and
- another interview to do tomorrow.

What do we do now to pull it all together?

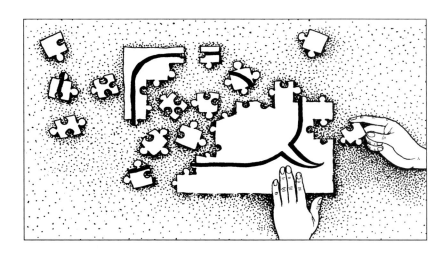

The Consolidation and Review Process

This chapter addresses the post-interview period. Far from being nearly over, the real work is about to start – getting to grips with what was said in the interview. The consolidation and review process, which allows you to make the most of what you have learned, involves the following steps:

- review a copy of the notes, marking areas that may need clarification
- walk through the notes with the interview team and reach agreement on what the interviewee said and how the business works
- fill in any gaps of understanding in the notes from memory
- use the tape recording to confirm understanding, where necessary, especially when the interview was done by one person only
- try to explain how something in the business works to other members of the project team– if you cannot explain it, your understanding of it is still incomplete
- note problems and use as questions for subsequent interviews
- resolve follow-up questions by telephone – except in unusual cases, only schedule another interview if the original one was interrupted
- write a summary of the interview notes (optional)
- annotate the interview notes
- capture extracts of notes in computer tools (or manual files)
- model your understanding – start to produce the structured models or add to those already created after earlier interviews.

Figure 8-1
Overview from Interview to Key Outcomes

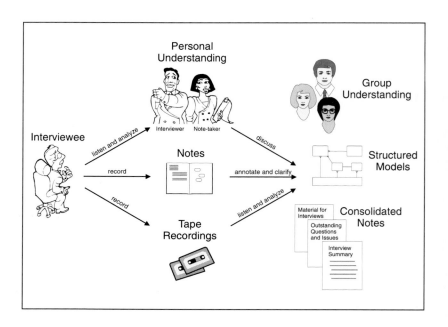

Key Outcomes

The formal and informal deliverables or key outcomes from the consolidation effort include:

- Your Understanding – at both individual and project-team level
- Consolidated Notes – both interviewer's and note-taker's notes
- Structured Models of the Business
- Outstanding Questions and Issues
- Preparation for Subsequent Interviews
- Follow-up Activities (e.g. collect a copy of the annual budget).

Let us look at the first three outcomes in a little more detail, starting with what you will understand as a result of an interview.

Your Understanding

Note-taker	*"There – that bit, where he said 'If the market were to turn downwards we would be severely exposed'. What did he mean by that?"*
Interviewer	*"I thought he was referring to the niche market – the post-retirement couples – that we were talking about earlier, and the exposure would be the amount of capital invested in machines to make the specialist products he was going on about."*
Note-taker	*"Oh, I see – but where did this objective of being able to reduce the amount it cost to retool the shop floor fit into that?"*
Interviewer	*"Well, that would make some sense then – if the cost were not so high for retooling, then exposure to a falling market would be less ..."*

This type of summary playing back from memory between note-taker and interviewer is a valuable aid to improved understanding and is especially valuable if it can be done with other members of a project team who were not present at the interview. The result will be a firm group understanding and additions to a list of outstanding questions and issues, which will help in the preparation of subsequent interviews. The written notes can be improved from memory during this part of the process. The most effective way, however, of improving your understanding is consolidating the interview notes and building structured models.

Consolidated Notes

The first time many of us take notes at an executive interview, we listen intently and write furiously for three or four hours without a break. When we look back at our notes, we find they are barely readable. They start off fine but deteriorate into a scrambled mass of hieroglyphics. And the batteries in the tape recorder have probably run out of power, we have not noticed (being too preoccupied with writing), so we have no back-up.

These notes are not going to be of much use to anyone. They will be of little use to the original note-taker, let alone anyone else, unless some work is done on them quickly, preferably immediately after the interview itself. Of course, there is always the option of listening to the entire tape recording again, provided the whole interview was recorded.

Some people like to use a hardback book for their notes, using one side of a double-page spread for notes taken during the interview and the other side for consolidation afterwards. Figure 8-2 below shows the notebook from Figure 7-1 on page 94 after post-interview consolidation.

Figure 8-2
Layout for a
Note-taker's Book

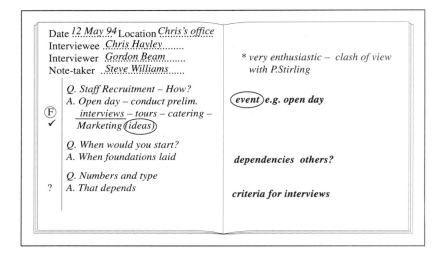

When you sit down to consolidate your notes, review what you have written. Are there points that you recall that are not in the notes? Close your eyes and visualize the session. Are there impressions or feelings that may be missing from the notes? Add any missing details. Perhaps early in an interview a term was used that was not known to you then – correct it throughout the notes or make a note in the margin.

Consolidation can start during the interview itself. Some people like to apply a level of analysis to what their interviewees say as they take notes by a simple highlighting technique. You can, for example, identify aims and objectives with rectangular boxes, key information with circles, business functions and processes with underlining and other items of significance with asterisks. This will give you a compact reminder of the interview and enable other project members to 'skim read' the notes to see what was said. You can also add colour coding with highlighter pens after the interview, but remember this will not work so well with black and white photocopying.

Figure 8-3
Consolidation during the Interview

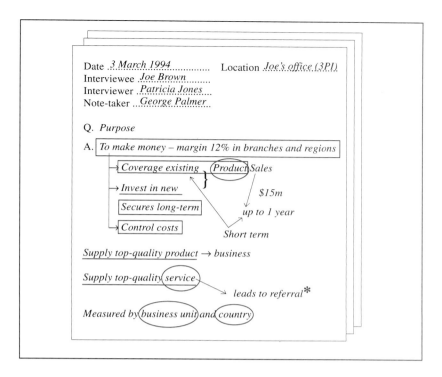

Date *3 March 1994* Location *Joe's office (3PI)*
Interviewee *Joe Brown*
Interviewer *Patricia Jones*
Note-taker *George Palmer*

Q. *Purpose*

A. *To make money – margin 12% in branches and regions*
→ *Coverage existing* *Product* *Sales*
→ *Invest in new* *$15m*
Secures long-term *up to 1 year*
→ *Control costs* *Short term*

Supply top-quality product → *business*

Supply top-quality *service*
leads to referral＊

Measured by *business unit* *and* *country*

Capturing the Consolidation with Tools

One technique that allows the whole team to have the results of the consolidated notes is to use computer tools during the consolidation session. We find this especially efficient when different team members are each assigned a type of material to consolidate. One person may, for example, maintain a file of business objectives, another person maintains a word-processor file on key information requirements (e.g. lists of business entities). These word-processor files can be easily reproduced – far easier than attempting to photocopy from a notebook with many topics on each page when one requires an extract of, say, **all** business objectives. There are various tools, including CASE tools, which assist in this aspect of consolidation. The advantages are many, including the ability to amend and update the extracts from the notes and ease of access.

Use of Tape Recordings

During the review of your notes, you will almost certainly find occasions when your understanding of what was meant is unclear – perhaps you learned something later in the interview which appears to contradict something said earlier, or perhaps it is as simple as being unable to read your own notes! This is where a tape recording is a useful aid to clarification. It should be possible to locate the relevant part of the recording quickly (especially if you kept time markers in your handwritten notes) and replay perhaps five or ten minutes of recording to clarify what was meant when the interviewee was speaking.

A word of warning: relistening to tape recordings can be an expensive use of time, so make sure that you do not continue beyond the point where it adds significant value. We have, however, found that listening to interview recordings is a very **good** use of time when travel between sites or commuting is necessary – especially as a way for members of a project team to hear what was said at an interview that they did not participate in. It is also useful as a way for new interviewers and note-takers to listen in on other people's techniques.

Another way to improve a group understanding is through the development of a set of structured models.

Structured Models

As a main consolidation technique and a fine aid to understanding, the development of structured models works well. We will look at three examples of developing scripts into structured models – models of objectives, business processes and information – and consider the value they bring to a project by way of understanding. (Appendix C gives a brief outline of these and other structured techniques.)

Objectives

Let us take the script from the previous diagram formalized into a set of business objectives:

Objective	Target	By (time)	Measure of Performance	Summarize by
Make money (profit margin)	12%	end of this year	100 × cost of sales/sales	branch, region
Maintain existing product sales	$15m	end of this year	total product sales	?
Control costs	?	?	?	?
Supply top-quality product or service	?	?	% recommendations, number of recommendations	business unit, country

This raises all sorts of questions:

What are our cost targets?

How do we measure the quality of a product or service? What specific targets have been set for this?

Are any of these objectives conditional on something external (such as a stable exchange rate)?

Do we need to summarize costs by branch or region? And if so, what do we do with costs that are not specific to a particular branch or region?

These questions can be used in follow-up interviews or questionnaires. Many of the objectives identified here will turn out to be relatively unimportant, although what a company measures certainly gives some indication of what it considers important. The most important objectives can be summarized into formal statements, for example:

To make 12% annual gross margin by the end of financial year 1994 company wide, assuming an exchange rate fluctuation of less than 5%.

A further level of detail showing how this can be achieved might be:

Figure 8-4
Details of One
Important Objective

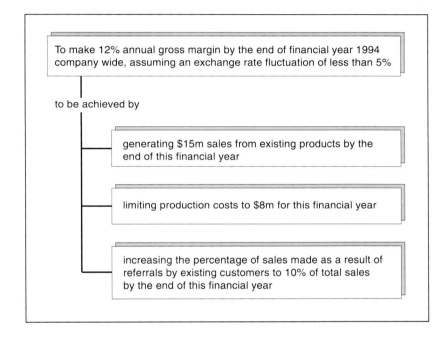

Business Processes

Of course, to achieve objectives, an organization has to **do** something. So what an organization does, business processes and steps in them, is also hidden away in the notes from an interview. These processes are usually signposted by a verb.

Figure 8-5 below shows a further section of the notes from the interview that we are consolidating. The answer to a question about what happens when a customer decides to buy something contains a lot of verbs, which have been translated into the initial process chart shown in Figure 8-6.

Figure 8-5
Further Example Notes

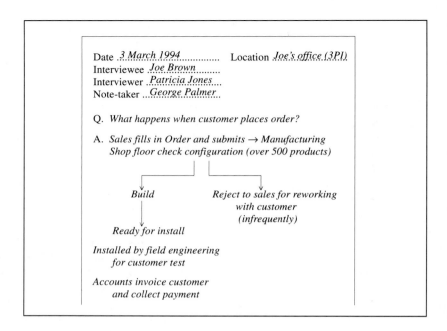

This might produce an initial process chart to cover the part of the business discussed in the interview.

Figure 8-6
An Initial Process Chart

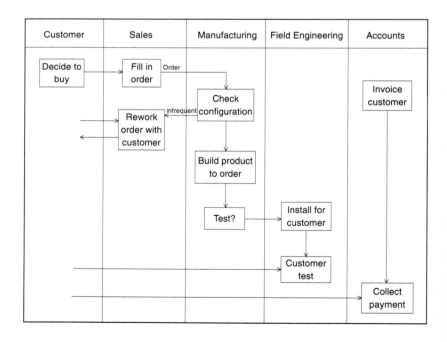

This initial order process chart is incomplete and will also raise questions:

What if the 'install for customer' process step goes wrong?

What causes the invoice to be raised? the receipt of the order? the completion of the product build?

These structured diagrams allow the analyst to see how processes relate (or could relate) to the business objectives. For instance, we have raised a question about what triggers the process to invoice the customer. If we delay invoicing until after a successful installation, that will help the perception of service quality; on the other hand it will also mean taking longer to go through the customer-payment process, so it may affect our profitability. A business decision may be needed to strike a balance between two **apparently** competing but desirable objectives – to provide a top-quality service and to be profitable.

Information Models

An initial information (or data) model in the form of an entity relationship diagram can also be built from this section of the interview script. (See Appendix C for a description of this modelling technique.)

Figure 8-7
An Initial
Information Model

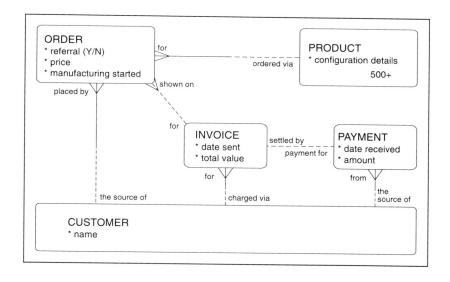

Once again, when the interview material is presented as a structured diagram, which after just one interview will be incorrect and incomplete, further questions will undoubtedly arise:

Is it possible to order more than one product at a time? If so, are the products always built and installed together?

Are invoices always settled by a single payment? Are invoices always settled?

The information model should provide details of all the information needed to support the business processes identified and it should also be able to measure the objectives modelled so far. The attribute 'referral' of the entity ORDER could be used for measuring the objective of 'Increasing the percentage of sales made as a result of an existing customer's referral ...' (part of the formal objective shown in Figure 8-4). Clearly much more information is needed for this one objective alone, and further deficiencies are revealed when the data requirements of the processes shown on our initial process chart are considered.

As you can see, these structured modelling techniques are individually powerful, but even greater strength lies in their combination to create a complete business model. Modelling business objectives identifies what the business wants to do and how it plans to achieve this; function and process modelling identifies what the business needs to do to achieve its objectives; and information modelling identifies the things it needs to know to perform these processes and measure its success in meeting the objectives. The models raise many additional questions, thus improving understanding of the business in a form that can be used by a project team and within the business, as a record of key elements of the business itself.

Incremental Changes to Structured Models

As each interview is held, more information is gathered and added to the structured models. If you are adopting a set of modelling techniques that are used to cross-check one another, then the amount of **new** information that comes out of the later interviews will be very small compared to what comes out of the early interviews. In fact, our experience shows that the profile of additional information in a set of models looks something like the graph below (also see page 52).

**Figure 8-8
Information Gained against
Number of Interviews**

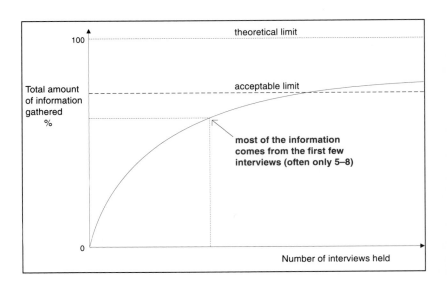

Other structured techniques such as collecting volumetric information, event modelling, matrices of various types, decision trees, summarizing issues and problems will be appropriate at different stages in a project (see Chapter 11, "Interviewing in a Business System Life Cycle").

Record Keeping

You can imagine how much information is generated by a series of interviews, which could number anywhere between six and fifty depending on the size and stage of the project. It makes good sense to catalogue and collect this information very carefully, either in sectioned-off files and a filing system, with spreadsheets and word processing, or with CASE tools that allow electronic access to the information as well.

Figure 8-9
Filing

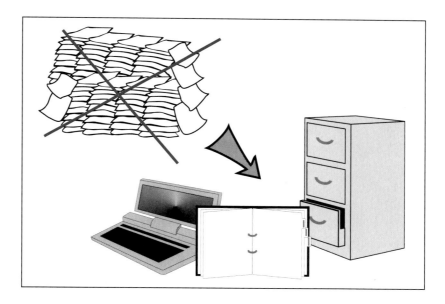

Most likely a combination of some manual and some computer support will be necessary for managing all this information. Make sure that you do not find yourself trying to design a filing system, as well as everything else, when you are half way through a project – do it before you get started!

A Note on Planning

Consolidation is important. **Plan** to do some. Most importantly, plan to do some straight after each interview. You may recall that the examples used in the chapter on interview preparation scheduled time for consolidation after each interview. The amount of information that you can recall after an event decreases rapidly over the first few hours and then levels off to a plateau after a few days.

Figure 8-10
Information Recall

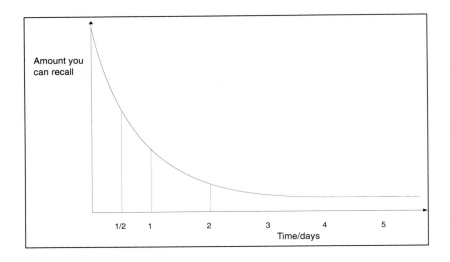

So there is no better time to consolidate an interview than immediately afterwards. The following diaries show some possible schedules for this:

Figure 8-11
Ideal Plan for a
Major Interview

	a.m.		p.m.	
Mon				Mon
Tues				Tues
Wed			Prepare	Wed
Thur	Interview		Consolidate	Thur
Fri	Model		Contingency	Fri
Sat				Sat
Sun				Sun

Figure 8-12
Less than Ideal but
Sometimes Necessary

	a.m.		p.m.	
Mon				Mon
Tues				Tues
Wed				Wed
Thur	Prepare		Interview & Consolidate	Thur
Fri	Consolidate			Fri
Sat				Sat
Sun				Sun

Obviously this second plan will put you under time pressure if you have to use it for a major interview. What if the interview is extended? Rather than leaving consolidation until the following day, do a first pass into the evening of the interview day when things are still fresh in your mind.

Figure 8-13
One to Avoid

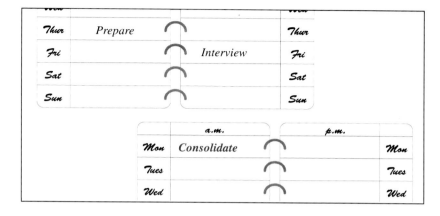

Here, there is too much happening between preparing for the interview and conducting it, and sufficient time to forget things before they are consolidated. The last scenario is just as bad. Not only is there a delay between the three stages for each interview, but there is a risk of remembering things from the wrong interview.

Figure 8-14
One to Avoid

	a.m.		p.m.	
Mon				Mon
Tues				Tues
Wed	Prepare 1		Prepare 2	Wed
Thur	Interview 1		Interview 2	Thur
Fri	Consolidate 1		Consolidate 2	Fri
Sat				Sat
Sun				Sun

However, it is not always possible to have a perfect schedule, and especially when dealing with busy senior managers some less than ideal scheduling is almost inevitable.

Summary

Schedule time to consolidate. Do it with the project team soon after the interview.

Aim to improve your understanding through discussion and development of structured models and use the consolidation period to fuel the preparation of subsequent interviews.

Devise a marking system for your notes to identify items needed for the models. With practice you will find you can do a lot of this analysis during the interviews. In this chapter, we used the following symbols when consolidating notes:

circles for key information, e.g. (Product)

underlining for business functions and processes, e.g. supply service

boxes for aims and objectives, e.g. control costs

and asterisks for other items of significance, e.g. leads to referral*.

A Practice Exercise

At this point, a short exercise will help you to practise these consolidation techniques.

Try taking the notes you completed after reading Chapter 7 (page 103) or alternatively those from the exercise in Chapter 4 (page 44) and consolidating them. You should as a minimum be able to highlight the significant phrases that describe business objectives, business processes and information. (Try the conventions illustrated by Figure 8-3.) If you have experience in structured modelling techniques, you might like to try to create some structured models directly from the notes.

9   ADVANCED COMMUNICATION TECHNIQUES

Introduction

Previous chapters have introduced and examined general techniques for interviewing. These techniques are basic and apply to most interviews. Improving upon basic interviewing, however, requires additional **communication** techniques. In this chapter we explore non-verbal communication during an interview and using it to improve the outcome. We then consider conversational style and 'verbal matching', which are closely linked to non-verbal communication concepts despite the apparent contradiction in the names.

Non-verbal Communication

Not communicating is impossible. Imagine yourself sitting in a restaurant observing others. Can you identify people who are business associates, long-time married couples, lovers, new acquaintances, family members? You can probably make very good guesses about many of them, but how do you know? Facial expressions, posture, gestures, eye contact and other more subtle non-verbal communication are clues that we are constantly observing. Many people do not consciously use the observations, but everyone has a subconscious reaction to the clues: it is basic in human communication – gestures and body language are referred to as the silent language.

Good interviewers use their skills in interpreting and responding positively to the body language of others. They observe the non-verbal as closely as they listen to the verbal replies. During an interview, the interviewee gives signals and constant subconscious reactions to the interview team. By responding in an appropriate manner, the interviewer can better control the results of the interview. Conversely, when the interviewer ignores important signals, the success of the interview is in jeopardy and good opportunities are often missed.

Many signals are sent during the course of an interview. The estimates given by experts in human communication are that humans produce hundreds of thousands of different physical signs! Even estimates of different facial expressions run at over 200,000 (Axtell, 1991).

Amongst the thousands of gestures and expressions, there are some common types that are of interest to an interviewer. The head and face are especially important during an interview, since a desk or table often partially obscures the hands, arms and legs of the other person. (Note that in popular television talk shows, guests are often sitting in open chairs – this is a setting that literally exposes them and prompts them for open responses.) Gestures play a major role in non-verbal communication, as they can provide important clues to inner reactions for experienced observers. Posture also provides us with further feedback.

This chapter provides only an introduction to a topic that can easily fill a whole book – with the intention of encouraging experienced interviewers to broaden their technique base still further. We will start at the top – the gestures and expressions involving the face and head!

The Face

The face is the primary focus of interest during an interview. Our faces change, in skin colour, expression and muscular tone, as we speak. Observe the face of a friend closely as you talk. The colour in the skin changes subtly to mirror feelings. Sometimes there is little observable change, but a sudden shock, anger or pleasure can be detected by changes in skin tone. Everyone has a personal palette of colours to express emotions.

Eyes play a very significant role in non-verbal communication. Eye-contact sends many messages or signals. These messages are created by the length and type of gaze, as well as the automatic responses reflected in the degree of dilation in the pupils. They can be interpreted as: I like what you are telling me; I don't trust you; I don't think you understand me; or any one of a spectrum of meanings. Significantly, messages and behaviour surrounding eye contact are culturally determined. In business situations in Western cultures a direct gaze is interpreted as signifying interest and a certain equality between two people. In contrast, in many Eastern cultures a direct gaze may be considered both rude and disrespectful. This is one small example of the need to take care when interpreting non-verbal signs. The typical experience of Western managers working outside their own culture is to be disconcerted when they cannot achieve the type of eye contact they consider appropriate for a good conversation. In an interview situation, we need to be especially careful of achieving the appropriate balance.

So, what are we looking for?

Gaze

In our earlier example of interviews for Atlantis Island Flights, we would expect eye contact to be used to show interest. If either the interviewer or the interviewee averts his eyes more than briefly, this could be interpreted as: he is ignoring me; she is not interested in what I'm saying; a rude person; a timid person who cannot look his manager fully in the eye, and so on. All these messages have one thing in common: they reduce the rapport between the participants in the interview.

However, in a business setting a very long gaze can be disconcerting. The interpretation of a long gaze varies with the facial expression too. Either the gaze is considered too personal and only appropriate for a social situation, or it may be a dominating gaze that tries to create a commanding position. As a guideline, try to maintain good eye contact about seventy per cent of the time to show interest, but break the contact from time to time to avoid unnerving or 'rattling' the other person.

Figure 9-1
Instant Empathy?

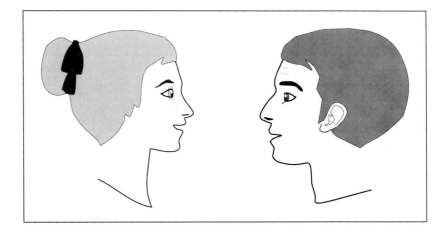

Dilation of the Pupils

Psychologists have documented a very interesting effect that occurs when eye contact is made between two people who have a personal interest in each other. There is an automatic response in the dilation of the pupils of the eye – larger pupils attract the observer. And because the response is automatic, we know that this is a signal with genuine meaning. The opposite message is conveyed by eyes with small pupils. In fact, it is an automatic physical response for pupils to narrow when a person is angry. The observer is both repelled and warned about the state of the other person. The old adage that 'the eyes are the windows of the soul' is based on such physiological responses which cannot be controlled but are completely automatic.

One useful general principle is that the shifting of the eyes carries meaning in a high percentage of people and some patterns exist. Eyes looking up towards the ceiling are a common sign when someone is trying to remember something (you know you have made the interviewee really think when your questions are greeted with a gaze at the ceiling!). Eyes looking down, however, are a signal that the interviewee is feeling under pressure or uncomfortable and may often be accompanied by a less than honest answer – so be careful how you probe on the topic that produces this response.

Most of our attention is directed to the eyes, but the rest of the face also contributes to the message. Eyebrows reveal interest, surprise and puzzlement. Our facial expressions are very plastic and the whole face conveys a broad range of meanings.

Head Position

Even the position of the head can tell us several things. A direct, open position (prepared to listen, prepared to participate) is indicated when the head is fully facing the other person. A head tilted slightly to the side shows interest and is a good signal for an interviewer to give to an interviewee. A downward tilt, on the other hand, can imply an aggressive stance, which does not invite openness on the part of the other person.

Gestures

There are thousands of gestures involving the face and head. A few examples should suffice to increase your interest in using and evaluating them.

Head

Negation and affirmation shown by nodding the head is quite basic. Be warned, though: there are cultural differences in the interpretation. A simple forward nodding of the head may signify 'yes' or 'I hear you' in some cultures, but 'no' in other cultures! In an interview, nodding the head is often an encouraging gesture as it signals general agreement and invites the speaker to continue. It also confirms to the speaker that the other person is actively listening, which is an important message for interviewer and note-taker to keep sending, both verbally and non-verbally.

Head and Hand

Other gestures involving the head and hands reveal some important clues. Stroking the chin (often accompanied by a frown) may be a signal that the observer is evaluating what you are saying. Holding the chin in the hand is more likely to signal boredom, a negative reaction or a wait-and-see attitude. Chin holding is not a gesture usually associated with action – consider the imagery of Rodin's famous statue 'The Thinker'.

When one or both hands rise to cover the mouth, the general interpretation is that a person is suppressing speaking out loud what he or she is actually thinking. This can range from simply concealing one's thoughts to masking a lie or hiding the truth. Closely related to this gesture of hiding the truth is a gesture of stroking the nose. For some reason that is not entirely understood, this may be an unconscious gesture made when someone is not telling the truth. This is an automatic reaction that most people are unable to control and, therefore, it is particularly useful in obtaining genuine feedback. (Investigators of criminal activity use these automatic responses to help them gauge the honesty of replies to their questions.) Of course, we must carefully reserve our opinions in using these interpretations; perhaps the person is simply scratching his nose!

Gestures, in general, are very spontaneous. The degree to which they are used varies from culture to culture and the type of setting. Gestures are used to accentuate a point of view – they emphasize the speaker's words or sometimes give a silent message when no words are spoken. Consider the rich vocabulary of pantomime, where entire stories are told through gestures. It is an interesting exercise to view a film or play in a language you do not understand and see how much of the plot you can work out on the basis of gestures and facial expressions alone.

In an interview, gestures give clues to the depth of feeling someone has for a topic. This is helpful in gauging appropriate responses. A question that elicits a strong response, such as 'no' accompanied by table thumping, may require following up to discover the reason the interviewee has such a strong feeling about a subject. It may also be a strong signal to tread carefully in the type of questions asked about that topic.

Some gestures are not quite so obvious and may even send conflicting messages. They may be different across cultural boundaries. A useful reference for interpreting gestures internationally is Axtell's book on do's and taboos of body language around the world (Axtell, 1991). A cautionary note should be added here – we usually **feel** the meaning of gestures and do not analyze them unless we are consciously observing a conversation. Nonetheless, understanding unconscious gestures will help the observant interviewer understand what is really going on in an interview.

Hands

The first impression we gain in an interview may come with an initial handshake. The personal variation and style of handshake reveals attributes such as interest in the meeting, need to control, status and similar personal characteristics. This flags some immediate appropriate responses, as well as indicating areas for caution. Have you ever shaken hands and been surprised at the limpness of the greeting? Your natural response is to try to raise the interest level of the interviewee in order to provoke a greater response. It can also signal that the person seems uncertain, perhaps about his own role or the purpose of the meeting.

Throughout the interview, the interviewer can learn from hand signals. Hands tightly clasped together show a closed or reserved attitude. This is not the time to expect agreement and it indicates a need to work towards a more open signal, such as open palms and relaxed hands. The action of clenching a hand tightly is often interpreted as defensiveness or even readiness to fight. A person will do this involuntarily, but it mirrors his feelings about a situation.

Directing the Interview

The interviewer should use his own gestures to help direct the interview. Open palms and a relaxed position invite open replies to questions. The interviewer also needs to display unaggressive hand signals. There are other simple hand motions for directing attention, such as using gestures for emphasis or pointing with a finger or pen towards a document or other item under discussion.

Be aware that your own body language will be interpreted by the interviewee. What will you do if you do not believe what you have just been told? Will your facial expression give you away? What will the interviewee's response be if he suspects you do not believe him? On one occasion, in an important interview, a relatively inexperienced note-taker heard the interviewee say something that was clearly inaccurate, which the interviewer had predicted during preparation. The note-taker flashed a quick and knowing glance at the interviewer with a slightly wry smile: the interviewee noticed, even though it took less than half a second. It was too late – the damage was done and some significant recovery work was needed to build up the interviewee's trust and confidence again.

Posture

Posture, or the alignment of one's body, exposes clues to attitudes and feelings, both individually and as the result of interactions between individuals. First, let us consider some common postural signals of individuals which are useful to note during an interview.

Is the interviewee shifting a bit restlessly in her chair? Body shifting tells us: I wish I were somewhere else. This may be a reflection of dissatisfaction with the interview or it may simply be a desire to get up out of the chair. The observant interviewer acts on this message and shifts attention to another topic, or perhaps suggests a physical break for refreshments.

How is the interviewee sitting? Is he sitting forward showing interest? This is a time to obtain personal viewpoints and commitment to an idea (salespeople are trained to wait for this signal). However, if the interview has been going on for some time, leaning forward with both hands on the chair may signal a readiness to leap out of the chair and leave the interview! Is the interviewee sitting back with crossed arms? This is a signal to proceed cautiously as the interviewee is in a closed position. At this point in time, he is not going to provide open responses. With arms, legs or hands in a cross-over position, the signals are closed in a protecting or shutting-out mode. An observant interviewer does not ask sensitive questions at this point, nor ones that need a candid reply. Instead, he asks general, objective questions, moving towards a topic that has personal appeal to the interviewee. Only when the signal of opening up is indicated by a movement from crossed arms and legs to a relaxed and open position will the interviewer attempt more sensitive questions.

Figure 9-2
Closed Signals
versus Open Signals

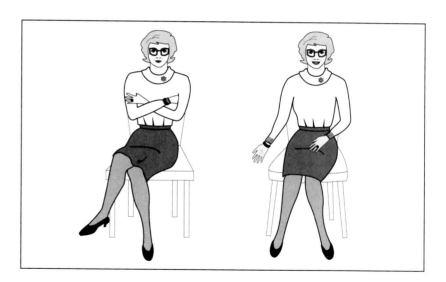

What are some of the dynamics in the interview situation which can influence such postural signals? There are several factors. First, the seating arrangement can help to avoid producing closed feelings. In Chapter 3 we pointed out the importance of sitting in an informal triangle around a table, rather than in a confrontational setting facing each other across a large desk. When the seating arrangements are more open and less formal, it influences the feelings of the participants and therefore their responses.

Another factor is the posture of the interviewer and its effect on the interviewee. There is a human reaction of mirroring which occurs when individuals are in close communication. If the interviewer adopts a posture that is open and relaxed, it will usually influence the interviewee – slowly the interviewee will shift to mirror the position of the other. This can be complex though: it may be necessary for the interviewer to first assume the more closed position of the interviewee – in effect creating a mirror or match with that person – then, when that begins to take effect, the interviewer can influence a shift to another position, by subtly changing his own position. Needless to say, this must be done in a natural and seemingly unconscious manner or it will become a parody.

Figure 9-3
Mirror or Parody?

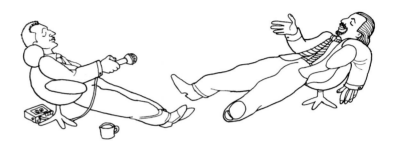

If you are conducting the session in a setting without desks or tables that could obscure a full view of one another, there will be a greater range of postural signals available for observation. Look at the position of feet and legs. Is everyone sitting in a relaxed open position? What direction are the feet pointing towards? We really do vote with our feet – they point in the direction of interest or preference. Have you ever observed someone hesitating to leave a room? The face may be turned towards others in the room, but the feet and torso are facing the door.

Seating arrangements influence other aspects of behaviour. The distance between individuals is important to their comfort. If people are seated too close to each other they feel uncomfortable, perhaps even overpowered. They will attempt to withdraw from such a situation quickly. The effect is even more dramatic when you observe people from different cultures standing and talking. Each person will be constantly asserting what he feels is the most comfortable distance. The striking result is that one person steps back and the other person then advances; if this continues for a while, one of them may travel the length of a room backwards!

Matching Conversational Style

Matching posture is a powerful signal in non-verbal communication. Desmond Morris has called it a 'postural echo'. However, another type of matching – conversational matching – can be especially important in an interview. Matching the tone and tempo of speech between the interviewer and the interviewee can make a significant difference in the ability to create and maintain rapport. There are many different conversational styles, but it is not often that we stop to consider how much difference there can be. The pace of delivery of words and thoughts can range from very rapid to very slow with long pauses.

In an interview, the interviewer should listen for the pattern of the interviewee and consciously make an effort to match it. One executive we interviewed had rapid-fire responses with many details and we knew that he would not appreciate slow, considered questioning – in fact, it would probably have made him impatient. So, we made certain that questions were posed in a similarly brisk manner. On other occasions, we have interviewed people who are slow to respond and who pause in their replies. For interviewees of this type, quickly asked questions could have the effect of freezing their ability to reply and, in the end, inhibit their answers. The interviewer needs to be sensitive to the appropriate style and be flexible in his or her own approach.

When the interviewee pauses in the middle of a reply, the interviewer needs to be careful not to interrupt inadvertently, as this can quickly lead to an awkward pacing in the conversation. People who speak rapidly are less aware of the length of time that some others naturally pause and they can anticipate the end of the statement too soon. On the other hand, some overlap can be tolerated, as in the case when one person agrees with a statement and chimes in to support that viewpoint. Judgement has to be used as the style of conversation varies, not only from person to person but across cultures too.

Matching tone can be slightly more subtle to observe. In general, we are listening for a range of loudness and the level each person considers to be appropriate. A soft-spoken interviewer may find his natural style is inappropriate when interviewing someone who speaks loudly. In this case the interviewer is at a disadvantage and the interviewee may try to take control of the interview because of the tone in which the questions are asked. The opposite case can occur if the interviewer is energetic and speaks loudly – a soft-spoken interviewee may feel overwhelmed or even irritated. In either case, it is the breadth of difference that makes the conversational style inappropriate for the interview. Skilled interviewers take note of possible differences and adjust their own style accordingly.

Verbal Matching

Psychologists studying rapport have discovered various matching mechanisms between people. The mechanisms may be non-verbal, such as those described above, or verbal. Verbal matching is selecting words that reflect the representational system of your conversational partner. In general, there are three representational systems called visual, auditory and kinaesthetic. Most people have a predominant personal system, which is reflected in their choice of words, as well as in other personal behaviour. If you concentrate on the choice of words of the interviewee, you will often discover clues for the representational system that dominates. So, what are the clues?

Visual

An interviewee with a visual representation system will use terms related to sight and seeing and images, such as *"I see what you mean"*, *"I get the picture"* or *"it appears to me"*. Visuals are graphically oriented; they tend to create mental pictures, memorize photographically and frequently select words rich in visual imagery. During an interview, such a person is likely to take up a pencil to draw a diagram or show an example.

Auditory

An auditory selects words that express sounds. Phrases such as *"I hear you"*, *"that rings a bell"* or *"I voiced an opinion"* may be used by an auditory. Such people love to talk and hear their own voices and words; they hold internal dialogues that go round and round (which can impede a decision) and select words that evoke sound. In an interview, they can easily be encouraged to talk and may need to be directed to avoid unnecessary repetition of statements and diverging from the point.

Kinaesthetic

The third type are kinaesthetics. These are people who get a feel for a problem. They require pauses in conversation during which they consider how they feel. They sometimes have difficulty expressing themselves in words and tend to select words that convey impressions. They might say *"I feel good about that"*, *"I grasp what you mean"* or *"I'll be in touch with you"*. Kinaesthetics, by nature, will be less forthcoming in answers to analytical questions, but will respond more readily to questions such as *"How do you feel about ...?"*

What is your dominant representational style? Most of us use a mixture of visual, auditory and kinaesthetic words and phrases; however, you can usually identify one set of words from the table below that feels more comfortable and natural to you. Listen to others in an interview – if you repeatedly hear words from one particular representational model this can give you direction for your subsequent questions.

Matching the style in an interview, a practised interviewer can select words that match the interviewee's dominant representational system.

This helps to improve rapport by increasing the sense that you communicate in a similar way. It also improves communication as well as the sharing of information by finding mutual grounds for expression. Of course, as with any technique, verbal matching is not intended as a simplistic solution. It is just one of the many ways in which we can create a comfortable environment for the interview. For example, if the person you are interviewing expresses herself as a visual, this may be an opportunity for you to use diagrams to discuss a topic. Ask the interviewee to show you the business units she usually interacts with. The resulting sketch may show some important relationships that would take much longer to describe in words. Use the sketch to ask more questions by building on parts of the diagram yourself.

We cautioned that an auditory can be someone who tends to be a non-stop talker who may repeat himself. This is a good type to reassure with the words, *"I **hear** what you're saying, could you **tell** me about ...?"* Controlling the length of response may be your challenge here, but it is also an opportunity to obtain rich verbal descriptions about a topic area.

The opposite case occurs with less verbally communicative people – the kinaesthetics. In order to engage them during an interview, use questions that draw less upon words and more upon actions and feelings. You could start a question with: *"What is your **impression** of the **move** towards ...?"* They may respond more slowly and pause frequently to consider their thoughts; this should prompt the interviewer to pace the questions accordingly. Consider shifting to a more action-oriented interview, one that has the person walking around the place of business in their mind or even literally, for example.

What you will be doing in each instance is matching verbs to the language used by your interviewee. Of course, many words are neutral and do not fit into any of these categories. The table on the next page gives some examples of words used by the three different representational styles to help you get started – add your own words to the list and try listening to an interview, such as a chat show, to get used to spotting the styles in practice.

Visual	Auditory	Kinaesthetic
perspective	listen	feel
see	deaf	touch
look	tune	grasp
view	note	handle
appear	accent	throw
show	ring	shock
dawn	shout	strike
reveal	dissonance	impress
picture	harmonize	move
clear	attune	grope
focus	growl	impact
envision, envisage	sing	hit
illuminate	sound	tap
twinkle	clear	hard
flash	say	unfeeling
bright	scream	scrape
outlook	alarm	suffer
foggy	static	tap
focused	rattle	rub
hazy	chord	crash
spectacle	amplify	smash
glimpse	overtones	sharpen
preview	clear as a bell	crawl
short sighted	express yourself	irritate
crystal clear	manner of speaking	tickle
imagine	rings a bell	sore
graphic	tongue-tied	grab
expose	describe in detail	carry
appears to me	unheard of	flat
eye to eye	voiced an opinion	numb
in view of	articulate	painful
mind's eye	vocalize	hold it!
see to it	hear	not following you
in light of	bang	come to grips with
plainly see	announce	get in touch with

(adapted from Laborde, 1984)

Practical Exercises

1. To use verbal and non-verbal clues effectively you need practice in observation. If you have not been aware of some of the signals in gestures, posture and verbal matching discussed in this chapter, start to look around you:

    –   observe the behaviour of people in a lift (elevator) – what do you see?
    –   in the next staff meeting, note the body language of each participant – what does it reveal?

2. It is especially valuable to observe a close friend or family member during conversations, as you know these individuals well and probably know some of their signals all too well but ignore many others.

    In the comfort of your family, try out your ability to create postural echo during a conversation. Do you find yourself matching unconsciously? This usually happens without your noticing. As you become aware of it, see if it is possible to effect some change in the other person as you change posture:

    –   when does this work?
    –   when does it fail?
    –   does the other person become aware of what you are doing? Ask.

3. Listen to your conversation with a friend or family member. It can be hard to do this – listening to your own conversation for both content **and** style – but persevere if you want to improve your interview technique. What differences in pacing can you hear?

    Now listen to the voice of a colleague – what differences in pacing from your own are there?

    Do you ever find yourself interrupting someone who is speaking? Listen carefully to the person's pace and pausing – perhaps the rhythm of conversation is misaligned – remember this also differs across national and cultural boundaries.

4. Another practical exercise is to turn the television to mute (watch the programme without sound) and concentrate on the non-verbal language aspects.

You will find that your observation and interpretation skills of non-verbal signals improve with practice. Try them out as appropriate interview situations arise and enjoy the full range of communication techniques available to an interviewer.

Summary

As soon as the general principles and techniques for interviewing are reviewed and mastered, there are some advanced techniques that you can add to your repertoire. The first section of this chapter looked at the strong influence of non-verbal communication and the method of communicating during an interview. Observing gestures and posture and being aware of matching verbal delivery are all elements contributing to advanced skills in an interviewer. Some practical exercises were then suggested to help build skills in this important area.

One important setting in which these advanced skills become significant is the workshop, or group working session, which is discussed in the next chapter.

Chapter

10

SPECIAL INTERVIEW MANAGEMENT

Introduction

This chapter looks at techniques for conducting interviews of three specialized types: workshops (e.g. for business process re-engineering), feedback sessions and knowledge acquisition interviews. In business process re-engineering initiatives, the need to collect information from a wide range of functional areas in an organization encourages an approach involving more than one interviewee per interview. Specialized techniques are needed for facilitating a group interview. Feedback sessions are another type of group interview used to check models built using information supplied by a number of interviewees. Knowledge acquisition in the field of expert systems, however, focuses very closely on detailed understanding of the logic of a single expert at a time. These three types of interview present a range of special requirements and they are dealt with here as alternatives to the basic one-on-one interviews.

Specialized Interviews

Information-gathering interviews may be held with one interviewee or conducted with groups in workshops. A workshop is led by a facilitator who manages the activities during the session and skilfully engages all participants in discussion. This role is similar to that of interviewer in the interviews described in the book so far. However, a facilitator in a workshop requires techniques in addition to those used for interviewing, in order to cope with a group of interviewees. Likewise, special methods are needed for interviewing an expert when developing expert systems. This rather specific type of interview uses some less well-known techniques labelled knowledge elicitation, which can also be used in general interviewing. We consider it to be another form of information gathering and have, therefore, included it in this chapter.

We will look first at the workshops, where a number of people are participating in the information-gathering process. Then we will look at knowledge acquisition, where an interviewer tries to acquire a very detailed understanding of one domain from an expert in that domain.

Workshops

It is often useful to obtain business information from a group of people rather than one at a time, but a distinction needs to be made between interviewing several people at the same time and holding a workshop where full participation of each person is the objective. There are two advantages to the workshop as a means of collecting information: firstly, it is possible to obtain a convergent view with participants selected from across the organization. Secondly, it is easier to see some of the more explicit political issues surrounding a topic. (That is not to say there will be full or honest disclosure!) Both views can be important for ensuring the success of a business project or initiative.

In this section, we focus on workshops established for information gathering and group action planning. Workshops may be used instead of, or as a supplement to, interviews in projects or tasks that require a group view, as they allow us to gather information rapidly and to work towards a group consensus. For example, business process re-engineering workshops promote the change management objectives of participation and communication of changes. As business process re-engineering is an approach for changing an organization across functional boundaries, it is essential for representatives from different parts of the organization to work together at the earliest possible opportunity.

Other types of projects can benefit from workshops as well. Traditional systems analysis often focuses on single interviews. Increasingly, however, workshops are being used for information gathering, as they can be compressed into a few days rather than over a longer period of time. The traditional interview programme is also dependent upon the availability of interviewees and the ability to schedule multiple interviews. Workshops themselves are not without scheduling challenges as **all** the interviewees need to be available at the **same** time.

Planning

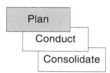

As an information-gathering exercise, workshops follow a cycle similar to general interviews: we plan, conduct and then consolidate workshops. First, let us consider the planning: we establish the objectives early – and notify the participants of those objectives in a memo confirming the workshop date. Here is an example from a business process re-engineering project for a metal trading company:

Memo

To: JL, PT, PS, MJ, MM, OS, MS, ST, AD, PL, LJ
From: PF (Project Sponsor)
Subject: Business Process Workshop (17 October)

Just a brief reminder about the workshop on 17 October and the objectives for the session. The purpose of the workshop is to identify the significant information, activities and processes required to support the business objectives and key measures of the organization. A model of the way things work currently will be created during the workshop. This is in order to identify improvement opportunities in the business processes. Your active participation towards that end is critical to the success of this session.

The session is an information-gathering workshop. The material will be consolidated by the project team and presented to all participants for checking at feedback sessions at a later date.

People are chosen to provide expertise in the topic being investigated and invitations are sent to each of them. In our example above, senior-level representatives from each functional area across the organization are invited. These include the financial director, controller, internal auditor, traders from different areas, accountant, commercial director, traffic manager, freight manager and director of information technology services (chosen using the techniques discussed in Chapter 5).

Figure 10-1
Attendees' Role in the Organization

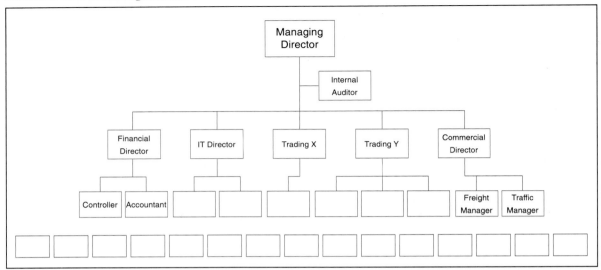

From our experience we find that a minimum of six and a maximum of sixteen attendees is a manageable number for a workshop. It is difficult to achieve a broad representative view across the organization with fewer than six. Also, as we often split the group into working sub-groups for periods during the workshop, at least six people are needed so that the sub-groups themselves are a sensible size. Working sub-groups are best kept to three or four to encourage active participation. The maximum of sixteen comes from the (sometimes painful) experience of managing even larger groups. We find it is better to hold several workshops rather than one with a very large number attending.

An experienced facilitator is critical to ensuring the success of the workshop. The facilitator achieves the workshop objectives through skilful guidance of the contributions of the participants, encouraging each attendee to voice views and provide input. The contributions are monitored by the facilitator, who is constantly scanning the group to engage everyone (interpreting the non-verbal communication is useful here). The content of the session comes from the participants. The facilitator needs good analytical skills and experience to respond quickly to the information coming from the workshop participants and guide the process – shaping the contributions without imposing his or her own judgements on any specific contribution. In fact, it is the facilitator that discourages any type of censure on the free exchange of ideas. Good facilitation is a mixture of interviewing, group management and note-taking skills, with the notes being kept on a flip chart, wallboard or overhead foil where everybody can see them.

It is often useful for the facilitator to have an assistant who is on the project team. The assistant helps monitor participation by encouraging additional comments, recording key findings (this is often done with software) and passing between the sub-groups as another facilitator.

Facilities

For a workshop to be successful, special attention should be paid to the preparation of facilities: rooms, environment, visual aids, stationery, and so on. There is a detailed checklist in Appendix D, but in this chapter we will concentrate on two major items – the rooms and stationery.

Rooms

If working sub-groups are planned, a separate room will be needed for each sub-group. The main room used for the general parts of the workshop which everyone attends can be used as a working room for one sub-group. This main room should be arranged with tables in a circle, square or U-shape to promote a feeling of equality and to make it easy for everyone to see a common point that can be used to project overhead foils, write on flip charts or point to pieces of paper. Figure 10-2 on the next page shows possible arrangements.

Stationery

As you can see from the suggestions for room layouts, various types of stationery are still the best way of working in workshops. Computer software packages and projection techniques will probably take over soon but, in the meantime, very effective use can be made of old-fashioned stationery. A word of warning: if you plan to use computers in a workshop session, do not rely on them! Have back-up in case the machine fails.

Paper

Use with small groups, where everyone can see what is being written.

Flip Charts

Use with any sized group. Make sure you have pens with thick nibs, so that everyone can see the writing. And remember to write legibly and in large handwriting – capital letters are best.

Overheads

Use with any sized group, although this tends to make the session feel more formal and presentation-like. Use overhead foils to jot down notes where everyone can see. Non-permanent water-soluble pens allow notes to be removed with a moist handkerchief if you make a mistake, although a stray finger or palm can also accidentally erase useful notes if you are not careful! Permanent pens are less forgiving, although more resilient.

Figure 10-2
Possible Room Layouts

Group Size	Arrangements	Comments
Small group (4-6)	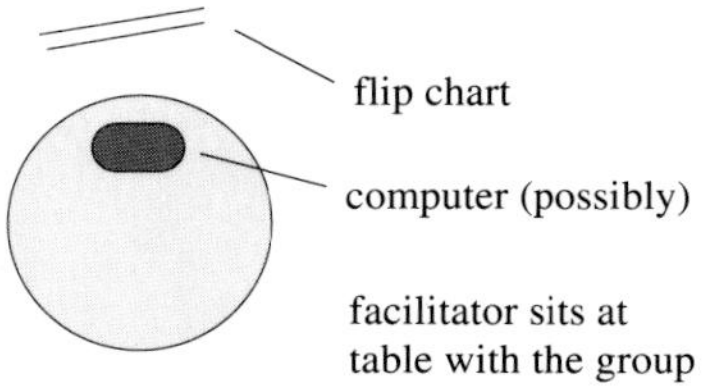 flip chart / computer (possibly) / facilitator sits at table with the group	Work done on paper and/or computer.
Medium-sized group (6-10)	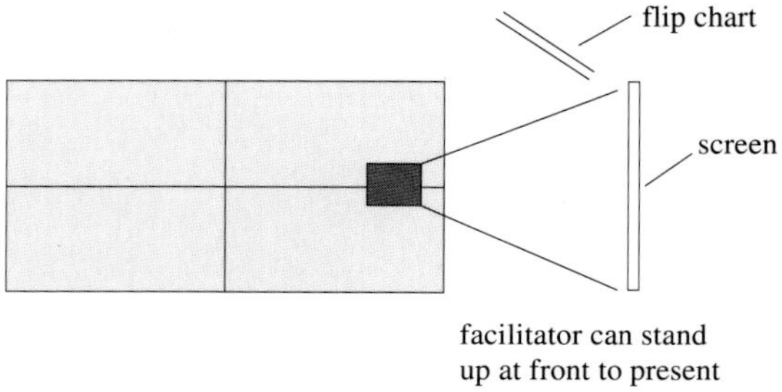 flip chart / screen / facilitator can stand up at front to present	Work done on overhead foils and flip chart or computer with projection facilities.
Large group 10+	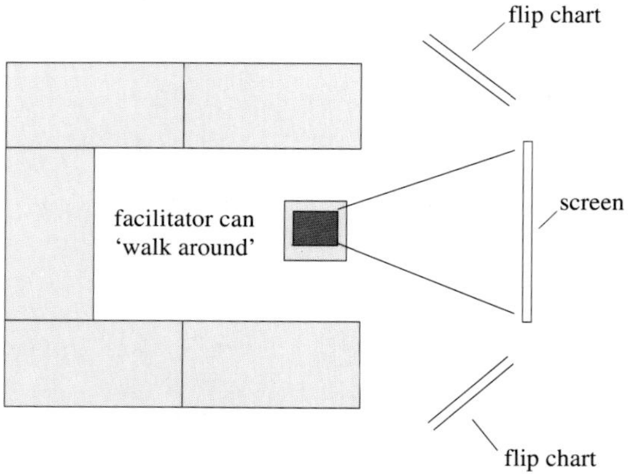 flip chart / screen / facilitator can 'walk around' / flip chart	Work done on overhead and flip chart only (write large enough for all to see!).
Working sub-group	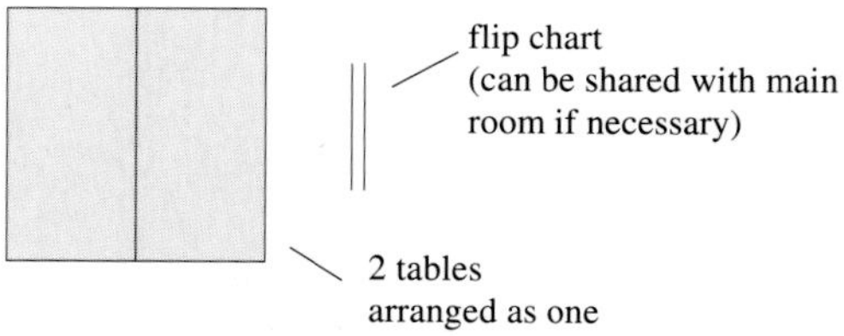 flip chart (can be shared with main room if necessary) / 2 tables arranged as one	Work done on paper and flip chart (and memo stickers) with some overhead foils prepared to 'present' back to the group.

An Example Workshop

If we take one example of a business processing re-engineering workshop, we can illustrate the skills and techniques used by the facilitator and assistant. In our example, the agenda is distributed before the workshop. It is divided into general sessions and small group sessions.

Agenda

General Session:
- Introductions
- Objectives of the session

Pairs/Small Groups:
- Identify business objectives/performance indicators and core competencies (strengths and weaknesses)

General Session:
- Discussion of group work
- Define the Basic business process

Small Groups
- Develop process map of existing process and identify areas for change

General Session:
- Presentation and discussion of each group
- Consolidation of the finding
- Define next steps

Breaks and lunches are set in a timetable for the agenda.

Conducting

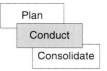

This is what happened during that workshop:

First the facilitator introduces the project team and attendees at the workshop. Sometimes it is wrongly assumed that everyone from the same organization will know each other, but introductions are always necessary, if only to more fully acquaint the facilitator with each person. One technique that is useful is to have each person briefly interview the person sitting next to him and to make the introduction of that person to the group. This helps break the ice and create a more informal tone, especially when a group is gathered around a table.

Then the facilitator briefly describes the purpose and objectives of the session, and asks for agreement from the group and suggestions for other objectives. At each point where the facilitator initiates a step in the process, general participation is then encouraged. One technique can be to ask each attendee for their expectation of the workshop and this may be included in the introductions.

The work tasks, such as the task of defining business objectives – an item on the agenda in our example – are all initiated in a similar manner. The facilitator first describes terminology to be employed and outlines tasks and the method of working. Then, brief examples are useful to initiate the work of individuals, pairs or small groups. The work tasks focus on capturing the required information so that any discussion point is recorded for later use. There are various tools useful for documenting ideas: overhead foils, flip-chart paper, memo stickers (the ubiquitous 'yellow stickies') or software. The basic technique is to employ the documenting tools continuously throughout the session – not merely as a summary activity, in stark contrast to meetings, where notes of a meeting serve as a historical reminder of the discussion, not as a tool for action during the meeting.

During the work on the tasks, the facilitator and assistant move between pairs or groups to assist. If the work is in a general session, the facilitator and assistant urge contributions from each participant. The facilitator does not give 'answers', rather the role is to assist in eliciting ideas and information from the workshop attendees.

In our example workshop, each pair or group is given overhead foils to capture their main points. Then the overhead foils are viewed in a general session. Discussions generate changes, which are directly noted on the overhead foils. In the first task, the group is moving ahead towards an accepted set of descriptive Business Objectives. In defining their Business Objectives, the group is striving to identify a common understanding of **what** the organization is trying to achieve.

The agenda then calls for a general session to define the Basic business process. Initially, the facilitator defines terminology and describes the process perspective, giving examples. Then the facilitator elicits from the group the core business process for the business. This is a horizontal view, one from the market outside the organization to the customer receiving goods or services. In most cases, some eight to twelve major process steps are suggested by the group. Here is an example from one organization.

Figure 10-3
The Trading Process

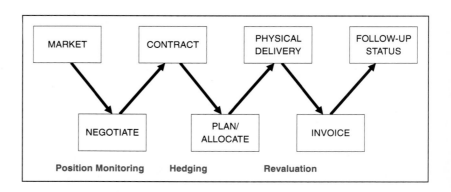

The workshop then breaks into smaller groups to refine the documented Basic business process (which was developed on an overhead foil and copied for distribution to the working groups). Working in small groups of three or four persons, the business process is outlined in more detail. The group works with large flip chart-paper and yellow stickies. They build a diagram sequentially of each process step. They note the information used at each process step. Next to the process step name (one separate sticker is useful for each step) participants write down suggested improvements (in red ink, perhaps) in the flow of the process. The improvements may be suggested for any aspect of the process. In one workshop, suggestions ranged from changing responsibility for certain work tasks to elimination of time-consuming procedures and redundant entry of information used throughout the flow of the process.

At the end of the work session, when the groups have all completed their work, each one presents its process diagram and key recommendations in a general session. The large group discussion aims at moving towards a consensus of the problem areas, priorities, and possible solutions.

The facilitator, assistant or one of the participants summarizes the findings and outlines the next steps. The next steps after a workshop will include consolidation by the project team, feedback sessions with the workshop participants and specific actions for each participant. One technique used is to have each participant state in a summary session what he or she will do to ensure specific agreed changes following the workshop.

Consolidation – Building on the Workshop

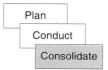

Consolidation tasks will differ, depending upon the work tasks undertaken during the workshop. The basic technique is for the project team to take the information from the workshop, combine it with other information sources, such as other workshops and interviews, and use the information for the next step in the project.

In our example, the output from each group is combined with the output from several workshops into an integrated process diagram. The work of each session is cross-checked and all elements included, in order to create a comprehensive model. The objective of the project is to improve the business processes and a key element is to rationalize the way that information is captured and used. The information requirements, therefore, are shown for each process step. In this manner, the point of capture for each item of information is easily identified so that this may be rationalized and the flow of that information through the process may be improved.

Workshop Software Tools

Workshops that are set up for information gathering and planning are increasingly using groupware, a type of software that supports the capture of ideas and information from multiple users during a workshop. There are some interesting techniques and methods available for the conduct of workshops using groupware. The advantages are many as the synthesis of multiple views can occur during the workshop rather than as a consolidation activity. A good example of the use of such a tool in a workshop setting is described by Eden (Eden and Ackermann, 1992), the creator of a method and the supporting software for group decision making on strategic issues.

Feedback Sessions

Feedback sessions are conducted at various stages of a project. A feedback session may involve a group of people for up to a full day. Participants are presented with the results of modelling, analysis or other project activities to date. The aim of feedback is to hold a working session to identify and correct inaccuracies and omissions in the models presented. To that end, the project development team should not be in **presentation** mode but, rather, in a **group interview** mode.

A well-run feedback session can be a major business benefit in its own right as it is a rare opportunity to take a step back and view what goes on across different functional groups in an organization (something rarely done by busy business people). In one feedback session with a freight haulage company where the board of directors were convinced that the right thing to so was to work out a 'fair' way to apportion costs for international haulage, a number of models were discussed. As the day wore on, it became clear to the participants that this was precisely what the business did **not** need. In fact, a scheme for apportioning costs would have resulted in a complex set of systems and would have detracted from the very objective they were trying to achieve, which was a more profitable **overall** business (rather than a number of apparently profitable businesses in each country). With this recognition, they reworked their process models in the remainder of the feedback session, achieving better **overall** profitability. This ended up with one country planning to run empty trucks more frequently than they had been doing to ensure trucks and trailers were in the right place at the right time!

Participants

Feedback participants are typically interviewees or participants in a previous workshop. The results of the interviews and workshops are consolidated, as we described in an earlier chapter, then the products of consolidation, such as models, are shown and discussed at a feedback session.

Objectives of a Feedback Session

Individual sessions will usually have one or two objectives unique to the session over and above the following general objectives:

- to gather more information from participants
- to identify and try to correct omissions or errors in the models and other project deliverables
- to agree words used to describe the business
- to agree actions to implement short-term changes where appropriate
- to gain consensus on the models and project plans
- to gain commitment to the project.

Planning

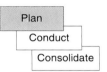

Preparations for a feedback session focus on ensuring total participation of the key users and a productive working environment. In many ways, preparation is similar to any interview but, in this case, it is for a group. The planning and preparation involves setting objectives, scheduling participants and facilities and preparing materials for use during the session.

After setting the objectives for the day, plan an agenda to achieve the objectives. Time management is critical, as the project team usually has a considerable amount of material to review with the participants.

A Typical Agenda

1. Introductions of Team and Participants
2. Objectives of the Session   Items 1–5 take
3. Review of the Objectives of the Project   perhaps 15–30 mins
4. Current Situation
5. Method of Working – Project Approach
6. Business Area – discuss 2–7 focus areas   )   bulk of the meeting
7. Next Steps

Scheduling

With so many busy people, it is difficult enough to schedule interviews and workshops at the beginning of a project. Consider what could happen if the feedback session were not scheduled early in the project. The session date should be set as early as feasible – usually a minimum of six weeks in advance – if the key senior managers are to be available on the same day.

Once the date is set and participation confirmed, facility arrangements can also be confirmed. Ideally, feedback sessions are held at off-site locations to minimize distractions. However, on one project, the entire Board of

Directors was involved and it was against company policy to have all directors off-site during a working day. The on-site feedback was shorter than most sessions as the need to answer urgent messages was closer.

The facility requirements include a room, audio-visual and electronic equipment, and catering for refreshments and lunch (if appropriate). Appendix D gives a checklist of typical requirements.

Preparation of Materials

In a feedback session the project team will show models or examples of the work to date. It is important that the feedback is billed as a work-to-date session, rather than as a final presentation. The focus of the feedback is current work and moving ahead on the project after the session so the materials that are prepared will vary from project to project. A typical feedback session in a business process re-engineering or system development project will work with the models and analysis produced from interviews and workshops.

If models are to be presented, visual materials that create a build-up of the entire model need to be specially prepared. It is never recommended to try to attempt to focus attention with a complete model. (The full model is a necessary reference item, but not the focal point.)

Communication theory supports limiting the items to be discussed or shown to between seven and nine discrete items. (This may be the number of bullet points on a slide, or the number of topic areas presented.) With a build-up of a model, the model is divided into no more than nine areas. A build-up, of course, provides a basis for chunking so that in the end more than seven detailed objects could be shown, as the observer will group several together by association with other topics. One example is the build-up of an information model (sometimes modelled as an entity-relationship diagram), where successive slides can show the key information areas, each containing from seven to nine objects or entities. In the end, as many as ninety detailed items can be presented, but in a gradual, logical sequence, which allows the participants to understand the whole **and** its parts.

For example, a business process may have ten steps in it and individual foils could be prepared to show:

1. the five steps in the 'usual case'
2. the additional steps that are done in the case of special customers
3. what happens if something goes wrong.

A critical part of preparation is to produce a list of outstanding questions for each area of a model or for other project products that need to be completed. We often use the technique of writing the outstanding issues or questions for the business area being presented on a blank sheet of paper placed behind each overhead foil (if other media are used, the same principle can apply). These questions provide guidelines for information gathering during the session. Feedback sessions can easily fall into a presentation mode, with little or no new information gained.

We are always asked if written materials should be handed out before a feedback session. In some companies, there is a policy of distributing an agenda and meeting materials prior to a meeting. We emphasize, in those cases, that our objective is to have a working session with the materials distributed at the point in the session when they will be used. We have found severe cases of misunderstanding if materials are handed out ahead of time, so we would recommend not doing so whenever possible. This can potentially disrupt and distract from the entire process of a feedback.

The type of handouts that are provided in a feedback are often written documentation – items that do not project well visually on screens.

Conducting a Feedback

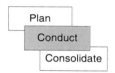

On the day of the feedback session one of the project team members can be the official note-taker. That person can also act as a time manager and provide a written summary of highlighted key points at the end of the session.

One objective, to gather more information, should guide the process on the day of a feedback session. For each topic area, which will typically be backed up with a portion from one or more structured models, questions guide the information-gathering process – they are like the checklists prepared for an interview. This partitioning into topic areas provides a semi-structured setting, is flexible and encourages the participants to provide needed information in their own manner. Example topics might be stock control, customer responsiveness, new product development and manufacturing.

Continual questioning during the feedback ensures that participants talk about seventy-five per cent of the time and the feedback team only twenty-five per cent. For example, during the feedback of an information model, describe the model using the syntax of the modelling technique and then question the names of the entities and relationships and ask for further attributes. Query for missing information and ask if there are any exceptional cases. The goal is to have a more complete model at the end of a feedback session.

Conflicting terms are used in any business. For example, what is an order? – it means one thing to a salesman and another to a production manager. There will also be issues that are still outstanding. For example, you may need to determine who is responsible for creating product codes. And is the same product code used throughout the entire business cycle – from design to after-sales – or are different codes used by different groups for the same product? Conflicting terms and outstanding issues can be addressed and often resolved in a feedback session, especially if enough people with the right level of authority to make changes are present. On the other hand, complex issues sometimes require a separate working session. Manage time and discussions by setting up an 'issues' board, which is clearly visible to all participants, and appoint someone to curtail prolonged discussion by recording the issue and perhaps allocating an individual to be responsible for following it up.

The attitude of the feedback team is important. Everyone needs to be in an open and learning mode and no one should adopt a defensive attitude towards the models or project results. It is important for the success of the project overall that the feedback is mutually satisfying. When someone makes a comment about an item, note the comment immediately and publicly on the overhead foil or paper copy being discussed. This technique helps to progress discussion and to focus on the points already agreed. Do not forget to carry the changes forward on items that appear on more than one overhead foil (e.g. during a set of build-up foils) or you will risk having the same discussion again!

Consolidation

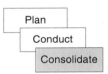

Time must be scheduled so that consolidation is done immediately after the feedback session. This is a time to take the overhead foils, flip charts and other tools used during the session with their comments, plus the notes from the feedback session, and make revisions to the models or other project products.

There are often follow-up working sessions from the issues board to schedule, as well as other follow-up activities. These need to be addressed immediately, while they are fresh in the minds of the participants.

It can be useful to send the written summary and key highlights to all participants as a record of the feedback work session. Again, ideally, this is done the next day.

Tips

- Schedule the session well in advance to enable full attendance.
- Plan a comfortable working area. Arrange seating to facilitate writing, revising, comparing – not in a formal presentation style.
- Make the user participants feel that they are part of the team – ask them to draw, write, demonstrate.
- Provide refreshments and breaks. Screen any possible sources of interruption. Consider an off-site location for the feedback to minimize distractions.

Knowledge Elicitation

Interviewing an expert to determine how that expert makes complex decisions and judgements is an activity primarily associated with the field of developing expert systems – systems that are programmed to make decisions using rules and knowledge in the manner of an expert. Medical diagnostic systems are one example where this technology is used. Because of the criticality of constructing an accurate model of the expert's use of information, the techniques for interviewing an expert have received considerable attention in the literature for many years under the term knowledge elicitation and, in general, are referred to as part of the process of knowledge acquisition.

Such labels have been sufficiently specialized to obscure much of the work from the view of analysts outside the field of expert systems. There are many parallels, however, to the objectives of the knowledge engineer (the person eliciting the knowledge from the expert) and any other interviewer seeking business information in a project or for the development of a business system. In the next section we discuss some knowledge elicitation techniques, which are equally useful in expert system development or other types of interviewing situations.

Each of the techniques may be used as the focus for one interview or combined with other interviewing styles described in earlier chapters. Many of the approaches used for knowledge elicitation are especially suitable for detailed information gathering. We will show how to use them as a means to confirm prior findings, or to clarify details. Several others are useful as a method for exploring a new area.

The field of knowledge elicitation offers an interesting variety of information-gathering approaches, far more than are usually described and used by business analysts, in general. They range from unstructured interviews ('ask general questions and hope for the best') to detailed grid and scaling techniques. The three-stage interview cycle (prepare, conduct, consolidate) applies in a similar way. First, do your 'homework' about the domain, the specific area of expertise of the expert, and plan objectives for the expertise-transfer sessions. Next, during the knowledge elicitation session, record the information manually or use tools to capture the logic of the expert. In the consolidation phase, the information is used to model the decision-making rules related to that area of expertise.

Knowledge Elicitation Techniques

In the preparation stage, **text analysis** is one technique for learning about the domain. Text analysis, sometimes referred to as lexical analysis, is especially useful for creating glossaries of a domain. Instructional and technical manuals are usual sources for such textual analysis. We can take a vehicle repair manual, for example, and extract key words, relationships, principles of repair, and rules for diagnosis and repair. The information derived in this manner can be used in later interviews to confirm understanding of the topic area or to consolidate the information to build a model of the repair system, in our example.

Several techniques require special advance preparation: **card sorting**, **twenty questions** and **questionnaires** are created before an interview session.

In card sorting, the interviewer prepares a separate card for each object or element of significance, then during the session, the expert is asked to organize the cards according to their relationships. The interviewer may choose an area for clarification. For example, with one vehicle manufacturer, in order to facilitate tracking one vehicle throughout the entire business cycle, the usage of different names for models of cars had to be re-examined. Each name is placed on a separate card, then each card may be arranged and rearranged to discover or confirm the relationships and associations between the items; for example, creating a tree structure (decision tree), differentiating between two cards, comparison between cards, and so on.

Twenty questions is useful as a confirming technique at a detailed level. With twenty questions, the interviewer creates a sample problem, often using one based on a decision tree that is being validated; for example, the medical diagnosis of a given disease based on responses to specific questions. The expert then asks twenty typical questions she would use to establish a diagnosis or solution for that type of problem. The response of the interviewer is always limited to 'yes' or 'no' in order to validate the decision steps. This approach is especially relevant for validating a model or decision tree for diagnostic process steps.

The use of questionnaires is often best limited to eliciting detailed information that does not require explanation. Information that needs further explanation is better gathered during an interview, where there is the immediate opportunity to clarify it.

The knowledge elicitation techniques chosen for use during an interview depend upon the type of interview: **unstructured**, **semi-structured** or **structured**. The unstructured interview is conducted in a free-association style and without any preparation or preplanned questions. As it is spontaneous, management of the material generated is especially difficult in the post-interview consolidation. There are large amounts of unstructured data to be organized. This type of interview is useful for courtesy interviews and for brief exploratory interviews.

The semi-structured interview is typical of the kind of interviews described in previous chapters. Checklists and objectives guide the predominant use of open questioning techniques. Within this type of interview, a combination of techniques is effective. One exploratory technique is to use **critical incidents**. The expert interviewee is asked to describe a critical incident or special case. This approach helps to elicit detail that often is not recalled as easily for normal events. A product recall is a traumatic experience in many businesses. Asked to describe a critical incident arising from a product recall, one interviewee provided important details related to normal processes which had not been discussed earlier. The approach often triggers new types of questions to ask about a topic area.

In contrast to the open questions technique, during a structured interview there is a strict agenda and lists of specific questions (which could be a questionnaire). The use of **repertory grids** and scaling is more likely to occur in this type of interview. These are tools as well as techniques from the field of psychology used for eliciting and structuring knowledge. The basic approach is to organize by pairs the elements or entities and those attributes which may be measured as ranges. (Attributes are qualities that distinguish and describe entities.) Entities may be ranked on a scale between the two poles of a quality, such as cost on a scale from inexpensive to expensive. In the example given below, we are seeking information regarding the rating of qualities for a pair of tools.

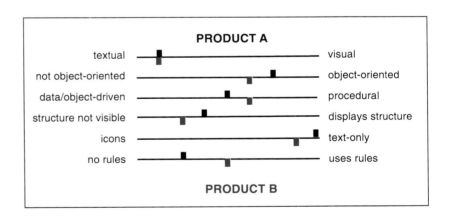

Figure 10-4
Software Tool Rating

This type of scaling can then be used to build a grid of attributes. If we adapt the basic principle, we can use the technique in detailed interviews by eliciting business entities and their qualities, then asking for a polar ranking by the interviewee. This enables you to build up a more complete understanding of attributes and entities (for example the viable ranges an attribute might take). Tool support is available to assist the application of these techniques in practice. There are many sophisticated analytical techniques, cluster analysis, multi-dimensional scaling and principal components, to name just a few, which may be of special interest to expert system builders as well as analysts seeking detailed specification of entities and attributes. An excellent review and bibliography of knowledge acquisition techniques and tools is given in Boose and Shaw (1989).

Another more structured technique is **scenario simulation**. In this approach the interviewer suggests a basic scenario and the interviewee verbally walks through the process towards a goal or until a conclusion is reached. Because it forecasts events based on a 'what if' situation, a scenario combines both objective and subjective information. This can be used to simulate the process of decision making used by an expert by means of a 'walk through' of the expert's reasoning process for solving a problem of a given type. This approach is useful, for example, for questioning an expert on details for diagnosing and solving technical problems. The characteristics of the what-if situation are outlined and then the expert describes steps to be taken and information required to reach a conclusion. Alternative scenarios yield different decisions and courses of action.

At the strategic level, scenario simulation is very useful in obtaining creative views on future events and actions. For example, a general manager tells us of a future state:

> *"Three years in the future ...*
>
> *"We are a subsidiary and internal supplier of electronic components to a large manufacturing company. We are creating a new local market and design products for local customers. We are establishing new business units and business processes – to develop and support new types of customers, to design innovative products, to market new products. Our workforce is in training for new ways of working, moving away from the more traditional assembly-line tasks and responsibilities ..."*

The differences between future and current provide the basis for many more detailed questions regarding what has to be done to achieve the future scenario. What kind of local customers do they foresee? How will they break into a new market? What business units need to be established?

Scenarios help elicit rich detail as well as the process steps and relationships of the elements of the scenario. This is a technique easily adaptable to a semi-structured or structured interview for many kinds of interviewees.

Observation rather than a formal interview is another facet of information gathering used for knowledge elicitation. The most common technique is

protocol analysis, which creates a 'think aloud' transcript. The expert performs a specific problem-solving task and describes each step and the rationale for taking that step. The transcript that is created is then analyzed, with the verbs providing identification of the operations/ processes and the nouns giving data cues. The analysis contributes to the model of that domain. Tape recording and videotaping are two common ways to capture a protocol. A variation of this is on-site observation with the interviewer watching an expert solving real problems on the job and recording the protocol.

> *The control room of a chemical processing plant is filled with monitors and screens. We watch the engineer respond to various data and alerts about the status of the processes. We record each action and frequently question why? and when?*

We can see protocol analysis as an especially good technique to employ for information gathering for business process re-engineering.

Lastly, the **Delphi technique**, widely used in strategic decision making, is of particular use in a multi-expert situation. The dilemma of how to gather and merge variations of opinion is always present in an organizational setting. The Delphi technique, named after the oracle of Delphi in ancient Greece, gathers information from experts independently, asking each one to rank or classify a strategic factor or factors, then the results are returned (anonymously) and the experts are requested to re-evaluate their earlier decision. This process is reiterated until a degree of consensus is reached. In our experience it very frequently occurs by the third round.

We used this on one project to predict and rank the strategic importance of offering alternative services to customers. Each expert was asked to express the importance of a particular offering, rating it on a scale from one to ten. On the first round, there was a wide spread of opinion. The results were tabulated and sent to the experts for a second opinion. The second round showed a movement of opinions and less gap between the ratings. Again, the results were tabulated without identifying the respondents and returned to the experts for a third vote. As you can see in the diagram below, after the third round, there is a fair degree of convergence, and the previous extreme values have moved towards the middle.

There is an element in human behaviour that seems to seek the median point! The technique is especially powerful as the political aspects of a source of opinion are masked. Similar results are reported by users of groupware tools, such as those developed by Eden (Eden and Ackermann, 1992). While the Delphi technique is not specifically an interview technique, it is an information-gathering and consensus-building approach of considerable power.

Figure 10-5
Typical
Delphi Technique Results

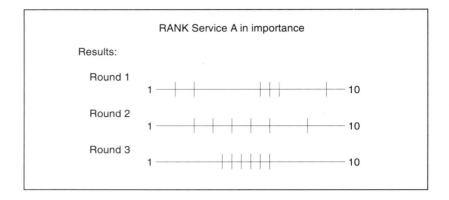

Summary

We have described specialized techniques for several special interview situations. The first type is the workshop with an emphasis on an approach used in business process re-engineering. Workshops require facilitation skills and additional techniques for information gathering. Team roles for facilitating workshops and a typical workshop are outlined.

Feedbacks are another type of group interview. Their special purpose is to obtain more information as well as to confirm the models and other products of the project created on the basis of earlier individual interviews and workshops. The feedback techniques described can be used for a variety of types of projects. They emphasize the principle of active user involvement in systems development, business process re-engineering or other types of business projects.

The third special interview situation is knowledge elicitation for expert system development. Despite a considerable literature on the topic, it is largely ignored by mainstream analysts. You can adapt the techniques for information gathering outside the arena of expert systems development. Critical incidents, scenario simulation, protocol analysis and the Delphi technique are just a few of the tools useful for guided information gathering.

11

INTERVIEWING IN A BUSINESS SYSTEM LIFE CYCLE

Introduction

A business system life cycle describes the phases that projects go through to develop business systems, from the initial need to ongoing operation of the system produced. There are almost as many variations of the business system life cycle as there are consultancy organizations in the world! And many larger companies have embarked on developing their own unique flavour of how to go about doing things to develop business systems – which leaves you with a bewildering range of possibilities.

This chapter looks at how to customize your interviewing technique for the stage of the business system life cycle you are in. We are interested not in the details of each step in any one cycle but in the characteristics of the interview situation you may find yourself in, so we offer general advice on how to plan and customize the interviewing you may need to carry out.

Let us consider three stages we should encounter in any cycle. We will call them Strategy, Analysis/Design, and Implementation: **strategy** is the early days of a problem (or opportunity), where people are trying to decide what to do about it; **analysis/design** is when a decision has been made on what to do in outline and some work has to be put into the fine detail of preparing to change the way things work; and **implementation** is the transition to a new way of working and a new status quo. In practice, things are seldom so clear cut. For example, you may think you are going to conduct a straightforward analysis/design interview and have prepared appropriate checklists and so on, but your questions may uncover vital information that could have a bearing on the whole system strategy. Obviously you are going to adapt your interview to this new situation.

These three stages can be thought of in any project, of any size. Even the smallest project has some form of orientation or getting to understand what is required; although the term strategy may be a bit too grand, the principles still apply. We have focused throughout this book on techniques describing **how** to draw out information in an interview rather than identifying **what** type of information to elicit for each specific situation.

Strategy – Early Days

Astonishing as it may seem, in many cases, projects are set up to be carried out as analysis/design or implementation projects without any strategy in evidence! In such cases, 'sufficient' strategy work is typically done as an early part of the projects in order to limit risk. This may involve nothing more than interviewing the project sponsor of a small project to short cut the process of articulating a coherent strategy. In these situations, this initial and often only interview is a critical part of the project, as it sets the scope for all the work that follows. Even small projects need a strategy and involvement from the right business people to be successful!

A Typical Situation

At this early stage, the problem/opportunity is generally not well understood – possibly it is not understood by **anyone**, and almost never by **everyone**. There is a rough idea of the scale of what needs to be done, but key players have differing views on the precise scope, degree and expectation of the results.

Some Examples

- Atlantis Island Flights wishes to diversify into the hotel business (except the Finance Director, who thinks now is the wrong time).
- A sudden change in exchange rates threatens a pharmaceutical company's overseas sales significantly.
- A nationalized industry is about to be privatized.
- A manufacturing company is losing customers to competitors with a strong customer service capability, so it needs to become more customer oriented.
- Your computer supplier has just withdrawn support for the computers that all your old and creaky systems run on.

Interviewers

In a large project interviews are partly conducted by the executives themselves in addition to the project team, although what they do is rarely thought of as interviewing, more as an exchange of ideas or testing a colleague's feelings on a subject. Many, but certainly not all, top executives possess the ability to listen effectively, which is a key interviewing skill. Strategic interviews are usually conducted by the more experienced interviewers, sometimes with external consultants to help out as well.

Interviewees

Executives

The executives are among the key candidates for interviewing as they are usually personally, and very closely, involved with the subject matter and stand to gain or lose most from the outcome.

Key Opinion Leaders

An expert, renowned leader or specialist in a relevant field: the opinion leader is worth interviewing both as a source of useful information and as a means of influencing the outcome of any project. This is an opportunity to get people who will make things happen in practice 'on your side'.

Customers and Suppliers

Including customers and suppliers on the list of interviewees can be essential, especially if the issue is one that has a direct effect on them. To limit time and expense, however, this is often done by questionnaires or telephone interviews rather than interviewing in person.

Industry Experts

Industry experts can provide valuable experience, from their knowledge of successes and failures of other companies in the same industry or even similar problems and opportunities from different industries. It is good to have a 'know-it-all' around if you have access to one.

Project Sponsor

Do not forget to ask the person who is footing the bill! Your sponsor will certainly have a view on what will be considered a success for the project.

Figure 11-1
Scope for
Strategy Interviews

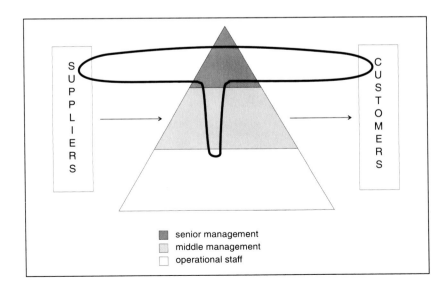

**Planning for a
Strategy Interview**

As this type of interview tends to be of senior executives, experts and people external to the company, such as suppliers and customers, the primary factor in planning is that of scheduling time in the diaries of some very busy people. These interviews also take a degree of preparation – background reading and so on (as discussed in Chapter 5) – and they produce a high volume of information to be consolidated afterwards. This means a planning window of up to two elapsed days per interview, requiring most of three working weeks to interview seven people (and that is if the interviews are scheduled end to end). The logistics for strategy interviews also need to be handled carefully, ensuring a quiet room, adequate refreshments, background materials and note-taking equipment (e.g. tape recorders, spare paper and pens, perhaps a flip chart).

**Conducting a
Strategy Interview**

Many projects do not have a formal strategy stage but the interview and project team should bear in mind the need to understand what the business strategy is. The aim, when interviewing senior executives, is to determine the business direction and seek opinions from key influencers. These people can also be used for testing your understanding. You could, for example, try the following hypothesis on a company with wide international interests: *"As exchange rates are fluctuating, I would expect you to tell me that you manipulate reserves of foreign currency as one of your critical activities: is this so?"*

Direction is provided through aims, objectives and a statement of purpose or mission. For instance, an executive in a company losing customers to its competitors may reveal: *"If we are to retain our position as the highest quality and safest provider of children's holidays abroad* (a mission) *then we must improve the way we handle the initial contact with parents* (an aim) *and we need to get our conversion rate from initial contact to serious enquiry up to at least one in five this year* (an objective). *"*

Finding a Mission

During interviews for initial, high-level studies, key words that are used to characterize the organization should be noted. If you ask the question, *"What is the mission of your organization?"*, and the response does not flow easily, the chances are that the organization does not have a formal mission statement. This signals a need for careful probing on the part of the interviewer. You could try asking, *"What is the central purpose of your organization?"*, or similar questions, at each interview. Familiar phrases will keep emerging, enabling the interview team to craft a single mission statement, which can then be checked out with the interviewees.

The following example is a statement of purpose for the diversification of Atlantis Island Flights into the hotel business, composed from the notes from interviewing the members of the Board of Directors of the company:

"To provide travellers, and the island in general, with premier, easy-to-use, local facilities, including conference, meeting and entertainment facilities."

At the time of the interview, various key words are used, such as easy-to-use, premier, top quality, localized and island community, from which the statement can be formed.

Conversely, if the question *"What is your mission"* produces a well-practised reply, or even a printed brochure with the mission big and bold on the first page, then it is worth testing to see how deeply people are committed to that mission (we are very suspicious about 'published' mission statements). Try asking, *"How does this mission affect what you do in practice on a daily basis?"*

Finding Future Plans

In a strategy interview, there is an ideal opportunity to understand future directions, by asking: *"What are your key business aims for the next few years?"* Record the comments, especially points given special emphasis, perhaps accompanied by a raised voice, sparkling eyes, enthusiasm, even desk thumping.

Examples of business aims identified from the Atlantis Island Flights project interview notes include:

- building a top-quality hotel that meets local, high, environmental standards
- gaining the lion's share of local conference business
- improving facilities for the non-tourist community.

The need to involve the top decision makers in the interview process for the study should be quite clear at this point. Only they can state what the business strategy will be in the future and they will all need to back the approach to make it a success.

Finding Business Objectives

The role of the interviewer is to ask questions that will elicit the necessary information for **complete** objective statements, so it is important to enquire carefully about the conditions under which the objectives will be achieved. Keep probing for quantitative measures. The vaguely worded statement, *"We want to increase profits"*, is investigated below:

Interviewer   *"How will you measure this increase?"*

Interviewee   *"We will measure it in terms of actual growth."*

Interviewer   *"What specific target rates of increase do you have?"*

Interviewee	*"We're aiming for approximately fifteen per cent per annum for the next four years."*
Interviewer	*"And are there any qualifiers regarding the possibility of achieving that target?"*
Interviewee	*"Well, if the economy remains reasonably stable and the overseas markets don't have any major disruptions ..."*

Probing, knowing when opportunities for exploring strategic questions are being presented, requires a skilful interviewer and good advance planning for the interviews. Your goal should be to sort out between four to seven key objectives at the top level (broad in scope, not departmental management objectives) which indicate the essence of the direction the business is heading in.

An Interview on Strategy Interviewing

This interview has a dual purpose: on the one hand it is simply an example of a strategy interview, while on the other it explains the purpose of a strategy interview, what the interviewer is looking for and how to achieve the objectives set for the interview itself.

Trainee	*"When you plan a strategy interview, what objectives do you set for the interview itself?"*
Expert	*"The major objectives are to:*
	– obtain information regarding the business direction; for example, mission, aims, objectives, business strategy, critical success factors, key performance indicators
	– obtain information to describe what the business does, or needs to do, to achieve the objectives and the key information the organization must manage
	– identify key business issues
	– gain some knowledge of the personality of the individual being interviewed and the politics and culture of the organization
	– establish commitment for the study."
Trainee	*"How do you accomplish all of those objectives in just one session?"*
Expert	*"By careful preparation before the interview and good management during the time available. You can see why four hours are usually necessary!"*
Trainee	*"In our interview with you last week, we discussed general interviewing techniques. Can you tell us what makes a strategy interview different from any other type of interview?"*

Expert	*"All of the general principles of interviewing are applied to accomplish the specific objectives of such an interview. Thorough preparation is especially important as the interviewees are usually top management. Someone at that level expects a significant result after committing four hours to an interview. The interviewer is concerned with obtaining all the information required to develop a good understanding of the business."*
Trainee	*"And how do you recommend preparing for a strategy interview?"*
Expert	*"Collect as much information as possible! Read about the company, the industry it is in, the product or marketing brochures, annual reports, business journal articles on the company, and any other sources you can identify. We usually ask the sponsor of the project to furnish us with internal publications, keep a watch for news articles in the business press, the Wall Street Journal, Financial Times, and so on, and use a business library or its equivalent for business background information. There are many excellent online business databases. If you can get involved firsthand with the company, such as becoming a customer for instance, this can be a useful source of understanding.*
	If the organization is in the public sector there may be fewer external sources of information, but usually there is more internal documentation available."
Trainee	*"What planning should be done for a strategy interview?"*
Expert	*"Quite a lot. I never like to underestimate the planning needed.*
	First: set the objectives, such as those we discussed earlier.
	Second: draw up an interview profile – know the interviewee's role in the organization, basic responsibilities, views and general background information, such as hobbies, to protect yourself against unpleasant surprises. I once found that the person I was interviewing as an expert had only been in the job for two weeks – an embarrassing lesson in preparation!
	Third: draw up checklists – have a general checklist for deriving the overall business direction statements and, for each functional area, have another checklist for that specific area.
	Fourth: consider questions for clarification and wrap-up.
	Finally: just prior to the interview, confirm the arrangements – date, time, place, refreshments, etc.
	It is often practical to split the interviews into more than one round, either running in parallel or one after the other. Usually, we try to limit the number if interviews to less than ten, but allow for additions to the list based on the recommendations of the first-round interviewees."

Trainee	*"Any specific recommendations for handling the actual interview?"*
Expert	*"Yes, establish a good rapport with the interviewee during the first few minutes – this is key to opening a good communication channel between the two of you. Use open-ended questions, based on the checklists, but allow flexibility in the sequence of the questions and let the topics flow naturally. Maintain control and steer comments back to topics when necessary, while remaining attentive and interested at all times – there is nothing worse than talking to someone who looks as though he is about to fall asleep!"*
Trainee	*"Are there any points on strategy interviewing we have not asked about and you believe we should discuss?"*
Expert	*"Yes, you haven't asked about the post-interview consolidating. It is important to schedule at least four hours for the consolidation as soon as possible after the interview. Take any notes and the tape, if you record the interview, and mark up the notes, adding to them from memory. We are looking for many things, so it is important to organize this task. I've found it helpful to look for the business direction statements and to indicate their location in the margin of the note-taker's notebook. Then highlight nouns and verbs that indicate information and processes in the business. It is useful to use colour coding for ease of later reference. Also note down other aspects, such as indications of the culture and politics in an organization.*
	I like to begin using structured business modelling techniques at this point and add to each model, after succeeding interviews, during consolidation – you can also use subsequent interviews to resolve queries and issues that arise out of the attempts to model the business."
Trainee	*"So, you work towards your final outcomes by adding to them after each interview."*
Expert	*"Yes, that's right."*
Trainee	*"Well, thank you for your time. This has been a very useful summary of a strategy interview."*

Analysis/Design –
Course of Action Chosen

Typical Situation

Between them, the group of decision makers in a company has decided on a course of action. This is described in some outline fashion and, while there may not be total consensus on this being the **right** thing to do, there is agreement that it is the thing that they **will** do.

Interviewers

Typically, dedicated project team members carry out these more detailed, fact-finding interviews. It is important that they are able to:

- communicate with a high level of language proficiency
- analyze business practices, procedures and transactions for the information content
- recognize the significance of the tasks observed.

The interviewer should have a clear understanding of the type of information to be identified and how to resolve ambiguities. For instance, it is important to know what a business process is (or is not!) so that it is clear when one is being discussed.

Interviewees

Executives

Re-interviewing key executives from the strategy stage can help. They have often been promoted up through an area of the company they know exceptionally well and have good ideas on how to change it. We once carried out a project for a transport company where almost all the Board of Directors had driven trucks for a living at some point in their lives, although this level of detailed knowledge tends to be unusual.

Middle Managers

Interviewing middle managers in order to include their views and gauge reactions is a key activity in a project.

External Advisors

It is usually possible to find a source of relevant information or advice, in the form of an external advisor, who is worth interviewing. This advisor may be a source of industry expertise, a customer, a supplier or someone from another company, not necessarily in the same industry (for some reason, it is harder to get the co-operation of competitors in this sort of exercise). Expect to reimburse the advisor commensurate to the time and expertise given. In some cases a consultancy fee will be appropriate, in others an acknowledgement in a report will be more suitable.

Specialists in a Specific Area

Most benefit comes from interviewing practitioners with responsibility for operations in a business area; for example, for a banking project, an experienced bank teller, the manager from a branch, a credit controller or similar. In effect, just about anyone can provide some information. It is, however, important to control the scope carefully, whether it be about the way some part of a business works currently or ideas and opinions on how it might work in the future. Note that Joe on the reception desk will quite readily spend all day telling you his life story, often adding very little value to the project.

Figure 11-2
Scope for Analysis/Design
Interviews

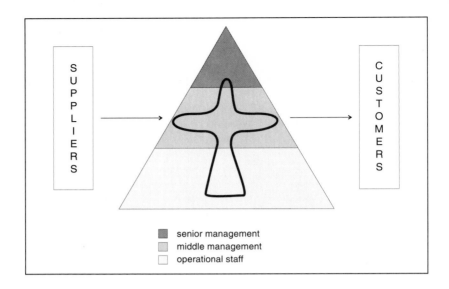

Analysis/Design
Interview Style

The aim is to build a more complete picture of the organization, its business functions, processes and information in **sufficient** detail to support the next stage. In practice, this means enough detail to make decisions on the type of skills and experience to recruit, the best way to design computer systems, the redesigning of a new product development process and so on.

Another concern is planning for the practical implementation of change, as well as gathering and developing criteria to be used to measure acceptance of the final outcome. For example, plans for training and education programs for staff and other long lead-time items need to be started early to avoid delays later in the process of change.

Interviews for analysis/design are conducted with representatives of three organizational levels: managerial, supervisory and operational. Different types of information are required from each of these representatives, as well as differing interview approaches.

The main objectives for the analysis/design stage interviews are to:

- determine volumes, frequencies and other statistics about how often things happen, how many of each type of product, service, document and other things of interest there are (focusing on those areas identified in the strategy stage as being critical)

- elicit detailed descriptions of what is done now, or needs to be done in future

- obtain sufficient information to understand the area of interest better than the person currently doing the job

– collect details about the information required to support these business processes.

Planning for an Analysis/Design Interview

One of the primary objectives for this stage in a business system life cycle is for the analyst to understand the area of interest **better** than people currently doing the job. To that end, the analyst needs to prepare carefully for interviews, as well as using other data collection methods.

A checklist of tasks to be completed during the planning phase for detailed analysis/design interviews would include:

☐ Review strategy deliverables

☐ Identify interviewees

☐ Schedule interviews

☐ Prepare questions.

Review Strategy Deliverables

The key deliverables from the strategy stage often include:

- statements of business objectives
- critical success factors
- key performance indicators
- a model of what things are done or need to be done (business functions and processes)
- a model of the information required to run the business
- an information systems strategy that outlines a proposed information architecture and development plan for the phased introduction of various systems.

Each of these should be reviewed by the analyst, especially if the analyst was not in the initial strategy team. For the best knowledge transfer, we recommend that at least one person from the strategy stage is included on the project team for this stage. Structured models and strategy reports can convey a lot of the information gained, but not all.

The basis for organizing information gathering at this stage is by business function or business process. The analyst will, therefore, need to review the functional models carefully – understand the links back to business objectives and critical success factors, and review the information needed by a particular function or process.

Identify Interviewees

A useful technique for selecting analysis/design interviewees is to draw up a matrix of business functions or processes by person, ticking the intersection where the individual has some detailed knowledge to contribute.

(Be warned, there are likely to be many more than in the strategy stage.) This will probably need to be done in conjunction with managers, who know their staff's skills and specialist knowledge, such as the example from Chapter 5:

Figure 11-3
Part of a Business Function to Person Matrix

Business Functions \ People	Parker	Singer	Evans	Black	Graham	Adams	Stirling	Slater	Fernandez	Schwartz	Cheng	van Velden	Hayley	Tracey
Establish schedule of flight														✓
Issue ticket for passenger*				✓		✓								
Check person in for flight*						✓								
Maintain standard fares	✓		✓	✓		✓	✓				✓			
Place advertising e.g. in newspaper		✓	✓											
Train staff							✓						✓	
Inspect/repair aircraft							✓	✓		✓	✓			
Refuel aircraft								✓	✓					

* priority from Strategy Stage

This matrix gives a good indication of whom to interview in order to pick up the detailed knowledge required. Note, especially, rows with only one tick in them, which may indicate a solitary expert or guru, and columns with lots of ticks in them, indicating a generalist or sometimes an opinion leader. A matrix can also indicate, by a lack of ticks, the areas in which there is a shortfall of expert knowledge.

'Check and Balance' Interviewees

It is useful to identify people in the organization who may be potential opponents to the project – people who are against the project and could disrupt or slow it down. Political or courtesy interviews will help them to become a part of the study, as well as provide you with an opportunity to secure their commitment and expose their reservations, so that you can alleviate as many as possible.

Schedule Interviews

A typical interview will last one or two hours (perhaps even less). There are more interviews to schedule in this stage and, usually, they are 'one-on-one' interviews where the interviewer also acts as note-taker. It is important to allocate planning and consolidating time, in addition to the actual interview time, and to allow a few spare interview slots, just in case some interviews need to be rescheduled.

Prepare Questions

The analysis/design stage investigates, amongst other things, the detailed requirements for proposed systems. The investigation is by business function and, for each function, it is necessary to prepare questions about:

- triggers (what causes the process to start?)
- function frequencies (how often is this done?)
- location (where is this done?)
- what is the detailed logic for the function?
- performance requirements of the business process: urgency, frequency, best-time and worst-time tolerances
- entities/volumes (details of the information needed by the business)
- attributes/domains
- relationships
- data location (where the data is currently kept, where it **needs** to be kept)
- data retention (how long is the data needed after it is captured?)
- transition issues (for instance, when is it possible or impossible to change over to a new way of working?)
- elementary business functions.

Detailed definitions of these modelling terms can be found in the glossary and in the other books in the CASE Method series, particularly the Function and Process Modelling and Entity Modelling books.

Conducting an Analysis/Design Interview

There is usually a combination of approaches for analysis/design interviews: dialogues are used for some, but interviewers also rely more heavily on directed questioning and on observation and prototyping as basic techniques. For example, it is quite common to conduct an interview while the person is doing his or her job, observing what is happening and asking questions as you go along:

- after a telephone call from an irate customer, you may say – *"That didn't sound very pleasant! How many calls are like that one?"*

- filling in an order form – *"And how many of these do you get through in a day?"*

- after discussing the way something **could** work – *"Why don't we put together a small mock-up of that so you can show me what you mean."*

Note that it is particularly useful to keep copies of documents and papers that you come across during these interviews for later analysis. We find that out of, say, one hundred documents, we might only use three or four for any kind of detailed inspection, but collecting copies at source can save substantial amounts of time in the cases where they are needed.

On the subject of documents, an interesting workshop technique that can be used with detailed group interviews is to draw out an entire business process (wall sized!) with photocopies of the forms pinned to the wall where they are used to communicate information between individual steps of the process. This can then be used as a discussion point, which can help tremendously when trying to come up with ideas for new ways of doing things.

An Interview On Analysis/Design Interviewing

Trainee

"What are the key objectives for an interview during analysis/ design?"

Expert

"The key objectives are to gather detailed requirements about business functions or processes and the information needed to support them and to identify transition requirements and constraints. This means that we need to collect complete information on all functions or processes, through to the elementary level, and full descriptions of attributes and domains for entities. We need to record metrics for business processes and entities; for example, how long it takes us to fulfil an order, how many customers we have. This enables us to complete the function and process models and a full supporting information model.

The purpose of gathering transition information at this stage is to decide on and plan for the changes we are going to make and to determine the requirements for the computer and manual systems.

Of course, the other key purpose of interviewing at this stage is to uncover some of the constraints and objectives of systems (particularly computer systems)."

Trainee

"Can you give me an example of what you mean?"

Expert

"Yes. There are always design constraints on systems; for instance, the cost to the business of the system not being available, or the level of security required to prevent unauthorized access to data. In general terms, interviews may be used to discover requirements relating to a system's:

- *performance*
- *back-up and recovery*
- *resilience and reliability*
- *timeliness of data*
- *security and access to the system*
- *availability (i.e. normal working hours for the system)*
- *flexibility to adapt to change*
- *overall size and cost.*

	These are business issues even though they can be quite technical as they affect the cost of information systems and the system's ability to deliver business benefit."
Trainee	*"We talked to you several days ago about strategy-stage interviews. How do these analysis/design interviews differ, apart from searching for some very systems-specific information?"*
Expert	*"There are significant differences in the type of people interviewed and the level of detail for the information gathered. Strategy interviews are driven by long-range business needs, whereas analysis/design is driven by business processes. At this stage, we are concerned with obtaining full information focused on the business processes and complete attributes for all entities, as well as the people and transition issues. Because we require details, operations staff are most appropriate as interviewees rather than the high-level decision makers interviewed previously."*
Trainee	*"What kind of planning do you do prior to the interviews?"*
Expert	*"We need to list session objectives, draw up interviewee profiles, compile checklists and contingency plans. At this stage, however, the interviews are shorter and more focused, so the preparation is commensurately shorter as well.*
	In preparation, review your strategy models and notes. In particular, re-examine the functions for which the interviewee is responsible or considered an expert or opinion leader."
Trainee	*"How do you identify the correct people to interview?"*
Expert	*"It is important to remember that this stage is driven by functions or processes. A good way to make certain that there is adequate coverage in the information gathering is to draw a matrix of people by process.*
	A few 'check and balance' interviews are also needed because there are inevitably people in the organization who need to be included in the interview process, but who are not identified as prime information sources. For example, it may be politically necessary to talk to a manager who is negative about the project."
Trainee	*"What types of checklists and questions do you recommend for analysis/design?"*
Expert	*"There are some major categories of questions to ask. Organize questions around processes, entities, sizing, people and transition issues, as well as the objectives and constraints for the system that we discussed earlier.*

For processes, determine all of the elementary processes, events that trigger functions, metrics for critical processes, and business units that are responsible for carrying out each process, as appropriate. Detailed information about the attributes of entities, the domains of the attributes and the designation of unique identifiers should be identified. The relationships between entities need to be carefully re-examined. Sizing questions are related to the frequencies and volumes elicited for functions and entities, as well as data location and data retention. (You can find some good detailed definitions of what is needed in the books in the CASE Method series, especially the Function and Process Modelling and Entity Modelling books.) People and transition questions cover a range of issues from end-user computer literacy through to transition windows and include discovery about the way the organization works, who has responsibility for what, people's attitudes and the culture of the organization – especially what will and will not be tolerated, degrees of change that are acceptable, and so on."

Trainee	*"What techniques do you use for the actual analysis/design interview?"*
Expert	*"I've found that a variety of approaches is useful at this stage of information gathering. If I only conducted dialogue interviews, I would miss an important opportunity to observe **what** has to be done in a business function and **what** the significant information in support of that function is. So a combination of observation and dialogue can provide more detail. Self-observation by the person doing the job can supply useful information, as well as observation by the interviewer. Prototypes can also be used as a vehicle for determining requirements and as a central point for discussions."*
Trainee	*"Prototypes at this stage?"*
Expert	*"Let me explain – the use of prototypes at this stage may be paper based; for example, showing a mock-up of a computer screen or a new paper form to see if all the right information is present. Another technique is to use storyboards to describe the order for doing the steps in a process. Of course, it is always important to be clear that these are not the final versions, but rather devices for feedback and discussion."*
Trainee	*"What are the quality control measures that you would apply to an interview at this stage?"*
Expert	*"That is an interesting question. Sometimes we fail to consider interviews as an activity requiring quality checks. Clearly, the most obvious check is: 'Has the interview achieved its objectives?' This check ensures we have set some objectives in the first place! Some of*

	these objectives may be fairly hard to measure, like 'have a good time' and I like, additionally, to have some checks on completeness, such as completing vital volume and frequency information on a specified part of a structured business model – for example, the number of orders that have errors in them."
Trainee	*"We've asked all our questions, so are there any other areas that you believe are important that we have not covered?"*
Expert	*"Just a final statement regarding the importance of cross-checking at this stage to ensure completeness. Earlier, I mentioned using a matrix to determine which people to interview and it is useful to cross-check each area of the analysis with these matrices: for example, functions or processes by entities, functions or processes by business unit, etc. There are now automated CASE tools that are invaluable at this stage, as handwritten matrices can be very tedious to produce."*
Trainee	*"Thank you again for your time. We will be meeting you next week to cover the topic of interviewing for the stages beyond analysis/design."*

Implementation – Making the Changes Work

Typical Situation

The course of action has been determined and details of what has to be done have been planned. Plant, machinery and systems have been bought or built, and the task at hand is to get it all to work together. For example, the hotel on Atlantis has been built, the fixtures and fittings are all in place, the computer systems are ready for final trials and the staff have all been through most of their training.

Interviewer

Implementation interviews are typically carried out by the people who will fix problems that arise, or by dedicated support staff whose primary role is to diagnose problems and then assign them to experts for fixing.

Interviewees

Implementation interviewees include systems users, senior and middle managers, auditors, technical staff, operations staff, and data and database administrators, as well as people external to the organization who are having to suffer the effects of the changes being made: in fact, everyone involved in the successful implementation of the proposed changes.

Figure 11-4
Scope for
Implementation Interviews

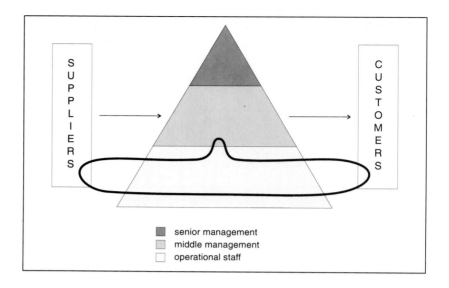

senior management
middle management
operational staff

Planning an
Implementation Interview

There are a number of circumstances in which an implementation stage interview may be held:

- a scheduled review
- an ad hoc review
- an unplanned problem.

Reviews are essentially events that set out to assess how well we have done against our original aspirations in a project. They may be planned or ad hoc, but are typically conducted as workshops requiring the advance scheduling and preparation work for such an event. Background information such as performance statistics may need assembling prior to the review, to act as discussion material. For instance, if we had set ourselves the objective of a three-day turnaround for answering customer queries, we could compile a report of the queries handled over the past month and the length of time taken for each one, with some summary statistics such as average time by type of query.

Unplanned interviews by their nature attract little preparation – especially if they are to deal with problems that need urgent resolution. Any support operative, however, will tell you the value of researching other known or similar problems with their cures. Basic checklists are still appropriate and in a system-support role, a checklist can provide a diagnostic aid. For problems with a piece of electronic equipment, a checklist would include such questions as: *"Does the machine have a power supply? Is it turned on? Has the problem happened before?"*

Conducting an
Implementation Interview

The interview process in the later stages is usually informal, but that does not mean it is unstructured or unplanned. It is important to create an informal tone and establish good rapport with operational staff, as both the user and system developer need to have respect for each other's knowledge. At this stage of implementing change, the interview is often by way of a review or audit of a system.

An Interview on
Implementation Interviewing

Trainee   *"What are the overall objectives for interviews at implementation?"*

Expert   *"The primary objective is to maintain significant contact with a system's users in the final stages of making it all work. In particular, to identify problems so that they can be fixed and to look for further improvement opportunities."*

Trainee   *"What methods do you use to meet the objectives?"*

Expert   *"Structured interviews play a less significant role. Dialogues are combined with other techniques, such as walkthroughs, reviews and feedback sessions for information gathering during implementation, as well as the more structured problem management process of logging and fixing problems with a system."*

Trainee   *"Does that mean there are differences in planning for interviews and dialogues for the stages after analysis/design?"*

Expert   *"The basic approach is still applicable: to plan the objectives for meeting with the interviewee or interviewees, prepare checklists and allow time to consolidate the information that has been gathered. The differences are in the means of collecting information, as I mentioned earlier."*

Trainee   *"Who will be the subjects for your information gathering?"*

Expert   *"The users of systems, people who have the task of making everything work in practice, are key contacts; also the technical and operations staff for systems, data administrators, database administrators and auditors, as well as specialists or experts in particular fields. Finally, customers, suppliers and regulatory bodies often have an interest in participating."*

Trainee   *"What are the core types of questions to be asked in implementation?"*

Expert   *"Questions are focused on reviewing the proposed processes and systems used in real situations. Once systems are in place and operational, questions for a system audit are the main focus. For example, reviewing how things are working in practice, whether the results are those expected – in other words, does the system work?"*

Trainee   *"Are there other suggestions for eliciting information from users and technical staff during this final stage?"*

Expert   *"We haven't mentioned attitude. It is always important in an interview to be open to the information that is being given. When system development staff conduct the interviews, walkthroughs, etc., a responsive, open attitude must be evident. The system developers should be genuinely seeking new insights on how to meet the business needs with the system being created and not be defensive. This can be quite difficult if, for example, you have spent two months working on part of a system that is disliked and is not working well. However, it is better to accept the criticisms and learn from them, rather than defend what has been done and incur the personal distrust of the people that have to use what has been produced.*

One of the main barriers to successful diagnostic work is the urgency with which people need, or want, problems to be fixed. Imagine you are measured on the number of orders cleared for dispatch in less than three hours and your main barrier to success is when part of a computer system keeps breaking down, causing delays to your order fulfilment process. These situations are often tense and demand speedy resolution. Good interviewing and diagnostic skills are invaluable here: imagine a meeting called to discuss such a problem."

The expert produces a well-worn scrap of paper with the transcript of an interview used to help people new to this type of diagnostic work learn new skills.

"Let's have a look at two different versions of the dialogue between the interviewer and the unhappy user."

User (angrily)	*We really need help with this *!@#! system; it is taking 30 minutes just to find free stock to allocate to an order even when there is plenty!*
Interviewer (defensively)	*Well, it's hardly the computer folks' fault; we have worked round the clock to get us this far ...*
User (even more angrily)	*Look – I have goals to meet and if you and your computer aren't going to help then as far as I'm concerned you can ...*

or

User (angrily)	*We really need help with this *!@#! system; it is taking 30 minutes just to find free stock to allocate to an order even when there is plenty!*
Interviewer (rolling up sleeves)	*That must be threatening your three-hour fulfilment goal. We'd better find out what's happening here!*
User (sensing at least an appreciation of her predicament)	*Too right we had ...*
Interviewer	*OK – show me what you have been doing and where it goes wrong.*

"The most professional interviewers start from the following assumptions:

- *the interviewee is right*
- *the interviewee is perfectly entitled to be dissatisfied with the way things are*
- *the interviewee is not attacking me **personally***

Often these things are not valid assumptions, but starting as though they are is more likely to lead to a successful interview, rather than allowing other assumptions and prejudices to influence the dialogue."

Trainee	*"That is a useful set of pointers. We appreciate the time and invaluable insights you have shared with us. Thank you."*

Interview Summary

Stage	Strategy	Analysis/Design	Implementation
Duration	3–4 hours	1–2 hours	$\frac{1}{2}$–1 hour
Level of interviewee	Managing Director, CEO Senior executives Industry experts Key customers Opinion leaders	Managers Key supervisors Operations staff (customers, suppliers and people in other companies)	System users Technical staff Auditors Data administrators Database administrators (customers/suppliers if appropriate)
Aims	Document business direction and enterprise functions/processes Produce an outline of the information required	Detailed knowledge of particular area Start to set expectations of what is possible	Validate work with users Present options to users Determine procedures to support the system Assess technical and audit requirements Evaluate system features Confirm transition strategy
Key types of information sought	Business mission Business objectives Core competencies Critical success factors Key performance indicators Business strategy Business functions/processes Business information Issues	Entities/volumes Triggers Elementary business functions Attributes and domains Relationships Sizing Data location Data retention Performance requirement Transition issues	Audit requirements Feasibility of design of back-up and recovery Issues and problems with practical use Ideas for improvement
Mechanism	Two-on-one interviews Workshops Feedback sessions	One-on-one interviews Prototyping Workshops	Review of new processes Review of new systems Structured walkthroughs Evaluation of prototypes Post-implementation review System audit Problem diagnosis Workshops
Types of question	Open Wide ranging	Open Closed, fact gathering Directed Observation	Diagnostic: *"Show me what you did"* Observation

References and Further Reading

References

Axtell, R. (1991). *Gestures: The Do's and Taboos of Body Language Around the World*. Wiley, New York.

Barker, R. (1990). *CASE*Method Entity Relationship Modelling*. Addison-Wesley, Wokingham, England.

Barker, R. and Longman, C. (1992). *CASE*Method Function and Process Modelling*. Addison-Wesley, Wokingham, England.

Boose, J. and Shaw, M. (1989). *Knowledge Acquisition for Knowledge-based Systems*. Eleventh International Joint Conference on Artificial Intelligence.

Buzan, T. (1974). *Use Your Head*. BBC Publications, London.
Published in America (1977) as *Use Both Sides of Your Brain*. E.P. Dutton, New York.

Eden, C. and Ackermann, F. (1992). Strategy Development and Implementation: The Role of a Group Decision Support System in *Computer Augmented Teamwork: A Guided Tour*, Chapter 19. Bostron, R., Watson, R. and Kinney, S., eds. Van Nostrand Reinhold.

Gratus, J. (1988). *Successful Interviewing*. Penguin Books, London.

Laborde, G. (1984). *Influencing with Integrity: Management Skills for Communication and Negotiation*. Syntony Publishing, Palo Alto, California.

Communication and Linguistics

Axtell, R. (1991). *Gestures: The Do's and Taboos of Body Language Around the World*. Wiley, New York.

Buzan, T. (1974). *Use Your Head*. BBC Publications, London.
Published in America (1977) as *Use Both Sides of Your Brain*. E.P. Dutton, New York.

Laborde, G. (1984). *Influencing with Integrity: Management Skills for Communication and Negotiation*. Syntony Publishing, Palo Alto, California.

Morris, D. (1978). *Manwatching: A Field Guide to Human Behaviour*. Grafton, London.

Pease, A. (1984). *Body Language*. Sheldon Press, Sydney.

Tannen, D. (1992). *That's Not What I Meant!* Virago, London.

Tannen, D. (1990). *You Just Don't Understand*. Ballantine Books, New York.

Interviewing and Listening

Boose, J. and Shaw, M. (1989). *Knowledge Acquisition for Knowledge-based Systems.* Eleventh International Joint Conference on Artificial Intelligence.

Buzan, T. (1988). *Make the Most of Your Mind.* Pan, London.

Evanson, S. (1988). How to Talk to an Expert. *AI Expert*, February:36–41.

Gratus, J. (1988). *Successful Interviewing.* Penguin Books, London.

Hoffman, R. (1987). The Problem of Extracting the Knowledge of Experts from the Perspective of Experimental Psychology. *AI Magazine*, **8**(2):53–67.

Prerau, D.S. (1987). Knowledge Acquisition in the Development of a Large Expert System. *AI Magazine*, **8**(2):43–51.

Business Information Systems Development

Barker, R. (1990). *CASE*Method Entity Relationship Modelling.* Addison-Wesley, Wokingham, England.

Barker, R. and Longman, C. (1992). *CASE*Method Function and Process Modelling.* Addison-Wesley, Wokingham, England.

Barker, R. *et al.* (1990). *CASE*Method Tasks and Deliverables.* Addison-Wesley, Wokingham, England.

Clegg, D. and Barker, R. (1994). *CASE Method Fast-track: A RAD Approach.* Addison-Wesley, Wokingham, England.

Strategy Development and Redesign

Eden, C. and Ackermann, F. (1992). Strategy Development and Implementation: The Role of a Group Decision Support System in *Computer Augmented Teamwork: A Guided Tour*, Chapter 19. Bostron, R., Watson, R. and Kinney, S., eds. Van Nostrand Reinhold.

Hammer, M. and Champy, J. (1993). *Reengineering the Corporation.* Nicholas Brealey, London.

Harrington, H.J. (1991). *Business Process Improvement.* McGraw-Hill, New York.

Hickman, L. (1993). Technology and Business Process Re-Engineering: Identifying Opportunities for Competitive Advantage in *Software Assistance for Business Process Re-engineering.* Spurr, K., Layzell, P. *et al.*, eds. John Wiley, Chichester.

Online Reference Guides

Dern, D. (1993). *The Internet Guide for New Users.* McGraw-Hill, New York.

Krol, E. (1992). *The Whole Internet User's Guide and Catalog.* O'Reilly and Associates.

Appendix

A

THE STORY OF A PROJECT

The following few pages chart the organization of Atlantis Island Flights, profile the key personnel within this organization and follow the history of a particular project – to build a hotel on the main island of Atlantis.

The Background

Atlantis Island Flights is a successful airline, established over thirty years ago, operating from the island group of Atlantis – in fact, it is now the main employer on the islands. Its founders, Lawrence Parker and Joe Tracey, are still with the company, although Lawrence is starting to plan his retirement. The company now wishes to diversify its interests by building a hotel on the main island.

Lawrence, the Chief Executive Officer, has delegated complete responsibility to Jill Graham, the Operations Manager, for getting this new project under way. The project represents quite a risk for Atlantis Island Flights, as it involves diversifying into hotel management, an area the airline has little or no experience in. It also involves a substantial investment and, on a small island, there is a high risk of failure unless the hotel becomes thoroughly accepted by the local community.

Profiles of Key Personnel

Lawrence Parker (CEO)

Lawrence is now sixty-five years old. He has nurtured Atlantis Island Flights from the very beginning and is looking to appoint his successor when he retires soon. He believes Jill Graham can do the job and views this project as a test of her ability.

Figure A-1
Senior Management Structure

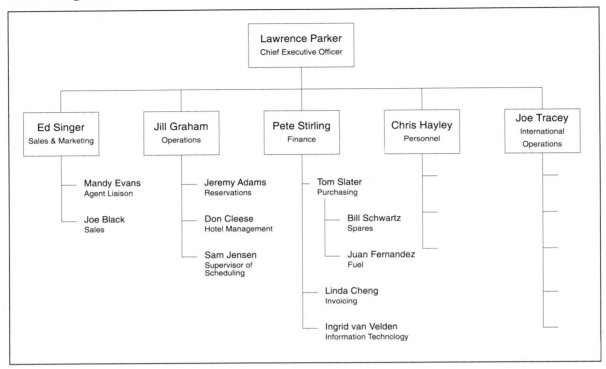

Jill Graham
(Operations)

Jill is young and ambitious. She has risen through the ranks at Atlantis Island Flights, having successfully run a promotions group in Sales and Marketing and the Purchase Division before her appointment to the Board four years ago. She feels that the company must change radically to secure its long-term future as an airline and also as the main employer in the islands.

Pete Stirling
(Finance)

Pete has been the Finance Director for nearly ten years and feels that the company should consolidate its existing operations before moving on to anything new. He disagrees with the project to build the hotel, as he thinks it will overstretch them financially. He and Jill are not compatible. Pete expects to follow Lawrence as Chief Executive when he retires, believing he is Lawrence's natural successor.

Ed Singer
(Sales & Marketing)

Ed is a young, go-ahead marketing executive. He is keen to promote the airline's services abroad to entice business travellers to fly with them from various places to Atlantis. He has a reputation earned from three or four highly successful promotions, including a joint project with a holiday resort on the main island, where they offered a package holiday in order to fill empty places on aircraft returning to Atlantis mid-week.

Chris Hayley
(Personnel)

Chris took the position on the Board with some trepidation, but has achieved the respect of her peers by establishing a number of popular travel benefits for members of staff. She has improved the complaints route for staff by establishing a special team offering a more personal approach.

Joe Tracey
(International Operations)

Joe has run this arm of the business since he and Lawrence founded the company. He inclines to a traditional style of management and prefers to have rules and policies to follow in his working life. He does, however, acknowledge the benefits achieved by the more modern, and sometimes unorthodox, outlook adopted by Jill, Ed and Chris. This does occasionally cause him some personal conflict in his work.

Consultants

Alan Scott (left) is the chief architect from a leading local architectural practice, Scott Design Ltd. Gordon Beam (right) is an independent consultant who has been hired by Jill Graham to run the project. He has worked for Atlantis Island Flights with Chris Hayley on a very successful personnel project and is already known and well respected within the company.

The Project

The idea of building a hotel is voted on at the March Board meeting. This is the start of a challenging two years for Jill and Atlantis Island Flights to develop and make operational a two-hundred-bedroom hotel with all of the associated systems, people and processes.

Having taken a month to set the team up, Gordon Beam holds two, half-day briefing sessions with the Board and most senior management, where the scene is set for the way the project is expected to work. They are all assured that their views and opinions are to be taken into account as part of the process. It is during these briefing sessions that Alan Scott and his team are introduced to the senior staff of Atlantis Island Flights. They have already toured the site for the proposed hotel with Gordon. This was an idea of Gordon's to ensure that the architects have an early introduction and a firm foundation to the project. After all, the timescales are ambitious to say the least.

Figure A-2
Project Plan

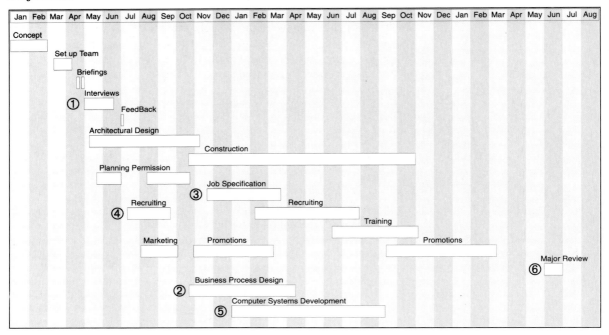

Gordon, Alan and the other members of the team spend the next six weeks interviewing the Board, senior management, key opinion leaders and other experts in various fields. After taking the individual views, they arrange a joint feedback session for early July.

Various discrepancies and disagreements are ironed out at this session and the team accepts one or two new ideas that come from having all the senior management in the same room at the same time. With a reasonably high level of confidence at board level, the architectural design for the building is then developed by Alan Scott. This signals the start of a scheme to secure sufficient funds to complete the project, as well as the building of the hotel itself. A programme of promotions from the marketing group and some detailed design of the business process that will be put in place to run the hotel also get the go-ahead.

By October, the foundations have been laid and the Personnel people start to put together job specifications and begin a recruitment drive to staff the hotel. While this is going on, computer systems are developed to support the staff in running the hotel and by the following June sufficient equipment and computer systems have been designed to start early training and education programmes for the staff involved with the hotel.

It is December when the Gala Opening Ceremony is finally held and the staff begin to run the Hotel Atlantis.

In June, a major review of the first six months of operation is held. The early operational problems are brought to the surface and the staff find ways of improving the services to customers, while correcting these problems. A subsequent review six months after that will reassess progress.

There are six places in the project where interviewing is a key technique (see Figure A-2).

- initial interviews and exercises to design business processes (1 & 2)
- job specification and recruitment campaign (3 & 4)
- computer systems development exercises (5)
- major reviews of the project (6).

Appendix

B   STRATEGIC DATA SOURCES

Strategic data sources are constantly expanding and changing. Data is increasingly available through online services. Access to the services will vary country by country. These are being introduced frequently, making it impossible to list all sources. We have suggested a few in the table on the next page and also provided references for guides to the international Internet for you to explore that rich information source.

General Online Services for

– Government data (varies by country)
– Online journals
– Online services: DIALOG, Reuters
– Online services connected to Internet such as Netnews

Internet is a part of interconnecting networks that collectively are referred to as The Matrix. The growth in information available is increasing at a phenomenal rate. To explore the types of service available, a guide is essential. For an introduction, see Daniel Dern's *The Internet Guide for New Users*, McGraw-Hill, 1993.

Other Sources of
Strategic Data

Business Press:

– Business Periodicals Index
– The Wall Street Journal Index US
– Financial Times Index UK
– Fortune
– Forbes

Industry Observers:

– Unions
– Chambers of Commerce

- International Organizations, e.g. OECD bulletins for member countries
- EU bulletins
- Watchdog Groups
- Central and Local Government
- Trade Associations
- Investment Banks

Data Source	Typical Data	Region	Online
Advertiser's Annual	general directory	UK	–
Business Information Yearbook	general directory	UK	–
Kelly's	general directory	UK	–
Kompass	general directory	UK	yes
UK Trade Names	general directory	UK	–
Jordan's	rankings	UK	yes
Times 1000	rankings	UK	–
Hambro Company Guide	financial	UK	–
Key British Enterprises	financial	UK	–
Macmillans	financial	UK	–
Stock Exchange Yearbook	financial	UK	–
Dun and Bradstreet	financial	UK	yes
Irish Company Profiles	company directory	UK	yes
D&B France Marketing	financial	France	yes
Qui Décide en France	executive directory	France	–
Hoppenstedt	financial	Germany	yes
Dun's Europe	financial	W. Europe	yes
Hoppenstedt Austria	financial	Austria	yes
Hoppenstedt Netherlands	financial	Netherlands	yes
International Dun's Market Indicators	sales	Global	yes
Canadian Dun's Mkt Ind.	sales	Canada	yes
D&B Canada Online	financial	Canada	yes
Moody's	financial	US	yes
Standard and Poor	financial	US	yes
Thomas Register Online	general directory	US	yes
Mergers and Acquisitions	financial	US	yes
Dun & Bradstreet	various	US	yes
OECD Main Economic Indicators	economic	Member countries	yes
IMF Balance of Payments	economic/financial	Global	yes

Appendix

C

BRIEF OVERVIEW OF RELATED TECHNIQUES

Business Direction Modelling

Business direction modelling is a structured way of modelling the future plans and aspirations for a business. Many variations of such techniques exist; most focus on what a business is trying to achieve, how it intends getting there and what may prevent it from doing so.

Concepts

Mission

What the organization is all about: the very reason for being there at all, what sets it apart from other organizations; for example, to trade profitably in foreign exchanges, speculating on future exchange rate fluctuations. For questions to get interviewees to articulate a mission, try:

> *"Tell me about the essence of your business as you see it."*
> *"What is the purpose of your organization?"*
> *"What is your company in business for?"*

Aims

An unqualified statement of intent, sometimes thought of as a 'fuzzy' statement of direction: for example, to improve customer satisfaction. For questions to get interviewees to articulate aims, try:

> *"What are you trying to achieve at 'xyz' corporation?"*
> *"What targets have you set yourselves?"*
> *"Tell me where you are trying to get to."*

Objective

A firm, qualified and measurable target to strive for: for example, to reduce personnel turnover to less than three per cent next year.

For questions to get interviewees to articulate objectives, try those for aims above, then perhaps having identified an aim or objective try:

"How would you measure that?"
"How will we know that the objective has been achieved?"

Strategy

A means of achieving an objective.

Critical Success Factor (CSF)

Something critical without which it would not be possible to achieve an objective.

Business Function and Business Process Modelling

Business function modelling is a way of modelling what a company does or needs to do to achieve its objectives. Full details can be found in *CASE*Method Function and Process Modelling* (Barker and Longman, 1992).

Concepts

Business Function

Business Function Definition

A business function is something an enterprise does, or needs to do in the future, to help achieve its objectives.

Business functions start with a verb and actively describe what is done, or needs to be done, using only terms in daily use in the business. The term 'business function' is often shortened to 'function'. Two example business functions are:

Agree the terms and conditions of a rental agreement with customer (e.g. hire charge, insurance cover) – from a car rental company

Set levels of taxation in line with government policy – from a government department.

Business Function Representation

A business function is shown as a softbox with its full name written inside the box, and a short name or label outside the top left-hand corner of the box.

Figure C-1
A Business Function

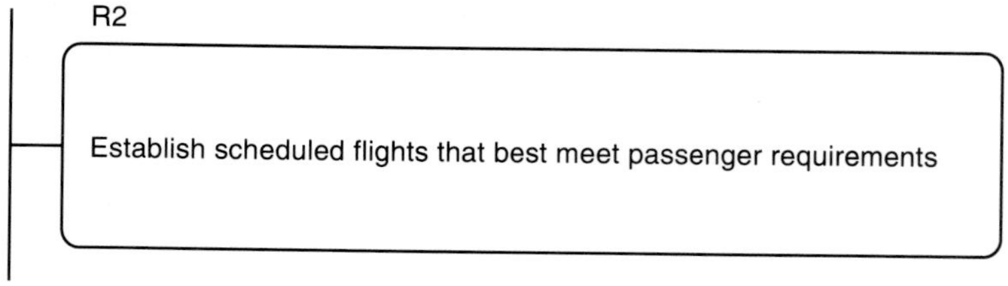

R2

Establish scheduled flights that best meet passenger requirements

Event

Event Definition

An event is a thing that happens or takes place or is an outcome or result.

It is the arrival of a significant point in time, a change in status of something, or the occurrence of something external, which causes the business to react in some way. We split events into four categories – external, change, time (or realtime) and system events.

Event Representation

Events are shown on function diagrams as hollow arrows, big enough to contain the name of the event, shown in bold italics. The arrow points at the function triggered by the event. If more than one function is triggered, the event appears at each function. Alternative representations may be used with CASE tools, as advanced computer-drawn graphics should be available.

Figure C-2
An Event

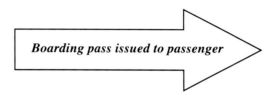

Boarding pass issued to passenger

Triggers

Events are important in function modelling because they trigger (or inhibit) functions. When an event occurs, it will possibly cause a number of business functions to be carried out. The arrival of the passenger at a check-in desk may cause three functions to occur:

Weigh, record, label and accept personal baggage
Allocate free seat to passenger for flight
Issue boarding pass to passenger.

Function Dependency

Function Dependency Definition

A dependency of one business function, B, on another, A, means that B cannot start until A has finished.

Dependencies arise for a number of reasons, including data, legislation and corporate policy. The easiest to understand is the data dependency: function A produces information needed by function B.

Function Dependency
Representation

Dependencies of all types are shown as a double-headed arrow between two function boxes. The function at the arrowhead (B) is dependent on the function at the other end (A), as on many flow-style diagrams you may be familiar with.

Figure C-3
A Function Dependency

Dependency, which means B must wait until the
dependency is resolved by A before it starts

Key Result

Key Result Definition

A key result is the outcome the business is trying to achieve upon receipt of an event.

Key Result Representation

A key result is, in fact, just another event and is represented in the usual way by a hollow arrow with the name of the event inside it. The result 'successful service of aircraft', for example, may itself trigger further functions.

Figure C-4
A Key Result

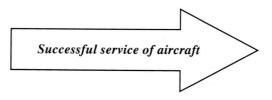

Successful service of aircraft

Business Process

Business Process Definition

A business process is a logical series of dependent activities that use the resources of the organization to create or result in an observable or measurable outcome, such as a product or service.

Business Process
Representation

Dependencies such as those described above are strung together in a chain in response to a triggered event to achieve some outcome described by a key result.

Figure C-5
A Diagram of a Business Process

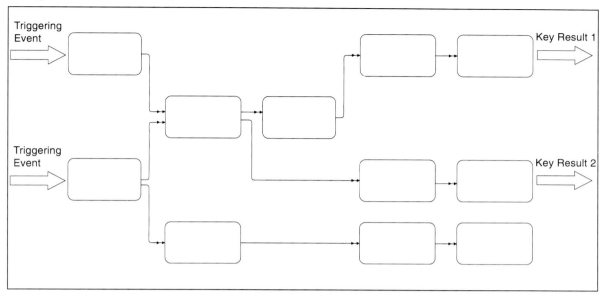

Information Modelling

Entity relationship modelling is a way to model the information needs of a business. For questions to get interviewees to articulate information needs and full details of the technique see *CASE*Method Entity Relationship Modelling* (Barker, 1990). In business information-gathering interviews, try asking:

> *"Tell me, what information would you need to keep track of to carry out your business?"*

> *"How would you measure 'xyz'?" (e.g. a particular objective).*

The answer will imply a need to know certain facts or items of information in order to measure the objective.

Concepts

Entity

Entity Definition

An entity is a thing or object of significance, whether real or imagined, about which information needs to be known or held.

Entity Representation

An entity is represented diagrammatically by a softbox (i.e. a rectangle with rounded corners) with a name. The name is in the singular and shown in all capitals.

Figure C-6
An Entity

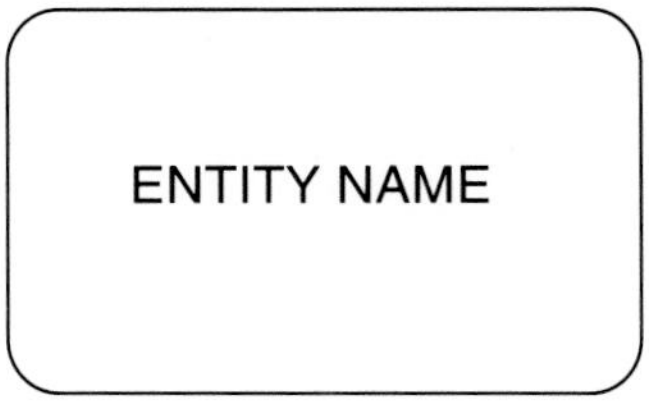

ENTITY NAME

Business Relationship

Relationship Definition

A business relationship, or relationship for short, is a named, significant association between two entities.

Each relationship has two ends, for each of which there is a:

- name
- degree/cardinality (how many)
- optionality (optional or mandatory).

Relationship Representation

A relationship is represented by a line that joins two entity softboxes together, or recursively joins one entity softbox to itself. The most common relationship is one that has a degree of **many to one**, is mandatory at the 'many' end and optional at the 'one' end as shown.

Figure C-7
A Relationship

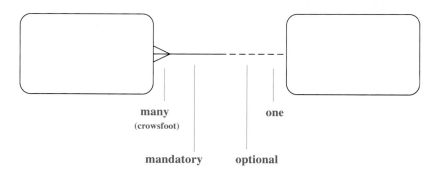

many
(crowsfoot)

one

mandatory

optional

Attribute

Attribute Definition

An attribute is any detail that serves to qualify, identify, classify, quantify or express the state of an entity
or
Any description of a thing of significance.

Attribute Representation

To represent an attribute, write its name in the singular in lower case, optionally with an example of its value.

Figure C-8
An Entity with three
Attributes

AIRCRAFT
registration number
date made
name

Unique Identifier

Definition

Each entity must be uniquely identifiable so that each instance of the entity is separate and distinctly identifiable from all other instances of that type of entity. The unique identifier may be an attribute, a combination of attributes, a combination of relationships or a combination of attribute(s) and relationship(s).

Representation

An entity may have more than one alternative means of unique identification. The primary method may be shown on the Entity Relationship Diagram by preceding an attribute that contributes to the identifier with a '#' mark and placing a bar across contributing relationship line(s).

Figure C-9
Unique Identifiers on an
Entity Relationship Diagram

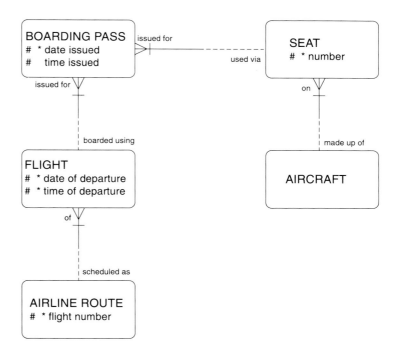

Appendix

D

CHECKLISTS FOR INTERVIEWING

The preliminary checklists provided in this chapter are designed for use as a basis for producing your own individual checklists for any particular project. If your interviews pass all the checklists, it only means they have passed the checklists. Do remember that checklists are a guide only and not necessarily a guarantee of a successful interview – good interviews will always depend on the performance of individual interviewers, note-takers and facilitators. However, these checklists will hopefully prevent you forgetting too many of the things that you want to remember.

Planning

The main difference between an interview and a casual conversation is the degree of planning; this is reflected in the size of the checklists given here for this subject.

General Checklist

Run through this checklist when you are setting up a project that includes a number of interviews:

☐ Is the purpose of the project well defined?

☐ Is the scope of the project agreed?

☐ Is it clear how the project will be measured for success/failure?

☐ Have you carried out the relevant background research?

– industry information
– recent company history
– current company position
– competitors
– products

☐ Are enough people being interviewed to cover the subject matter?

☐ Are too many people being interviewed? What would be the effect of removing some?

☐ Are any specific experts missing from the list?

☐ Will anyone be upset by not being interviewed?

☐ Have potential foes of the project been identified and scheduled to be interviewed?

☐ Have you scheduled time for:

– briefing (of interviewers and interviewees)?
– preparation?
– interviewing?
– consolidation?

☐ Are there a few free slots in case new interviewees are identified?

☐ Is there a time contingency if interviews slip or go on too long?

☐ Are the right interviewees being interviewed by the right interviewers?

☐ Have you allowed for travelling time?

☐ Are there contingency plans for an unavailable:

– interviewer (sick, injured, etc.)?
– note-taker?
– interviewee?

☐ Have you planned time for novice interviewers and note-takers to practise?

**Preparation for an
Individual Interview**

Use this checklist as part of the preparation for an individual interview:

- ☐ Do you know the goals of the interview?
- ☐ Is there an interviewee profile and have you read it?
- ☐ Is the interviewee still (after previous interview information) the right person to see?
- ☐ Is there a checklist for the interview – project and specific?
- ☐ Have you read the background material?
- ☐ Did the interviewee attend a briefing session?
- ☐ Has a briefing letter been sent to the interviewee?
- ☐ Do you know how you are going to start the interview?
- ☐ Do you know how you are going to run/structure the interview?
- ☐ Has a room been organized: ventilation, heating, lighting, seating, etc. checked?
- ☐ Have refreshments been organized?
- ☐ Have 'no interruptions' been requested?
- ☐ Have you reconfirmed that the interviewee has the interview scheduled for the right date, time and location?
- ☐ Is there a plan in case the interviewer/interviewee are incompatible? What about other potential problems?
- ☐ Have you checked there are no objections to using a tape recorder?
- ☐ Have you reviewed the issues that this interviewee may be able to resolve?
- ☐ Have open questions been prepared for this interview?
- ☐ Has the area for discussion been well researched?

Interviewing Checklist

☐ Professional dress and manner

A few keywords only have been given here – running through this kind of checklist while conducting an interview is the last thing you need!:

☐ Environment control (relaxed atmosphere)

☐ Peace and quiet with no interruptions

☐ Objectives

☐ Stay on track

☐ Add value

☐ Enjoy it!

Note-taking

It is important to be well prepared for the role of note-taker – notes are often the only tangible result of an interview:

☐ Ensure that there is access to a translator, if necessary

☐ Check that there is a tape recorder available and **working**, with:

 – batteries (including spares)
 – blank tapes (including spares)
 – a sound absorber to go between tape recorder and table top, e.g. a cloth

☐ Ensure that all necessary documentation is collected either at the meeting or beforehand

☐ Make sure that there is plenty of blank paper: preferably in a book; if loose paper, then pages numbered

☐ Make sure that there are spare pens/pencils

☐ Ensure that the checklist/questions are reviewed

☐ Be prepared to take over the interview, if necessary.

Techniques in Questioning

This list gives some techniques that you may find useful during the interview, especially if the interviewee is proving unco-operative or reticent:

☐ Have a polite interruption phrase ready

☐ Tour the business area

☐ Elicit details by example or diagram

☐ Elicit measures and objectives

☐ Reframe questions using examples and/or diagrams

☐ Examine documents together

☐ Work from real examples (e.g. the model of a product)

☐ Probe if you receive closed or defensive answers

☐ Confirm coverage of topics

☐ Ask for leads with regard to further potential interviewees

☐ Confirm their availability for the next step

☐ Summarize

☐ Use non-biased phrasing for honest replies.

Examples of Open Questions

Here are some suggestions for open questions. Do not use them verbatim: phrase your own questions or rephrase these to make them personal.

Strategic

☐ In your own words, tell us the essence of the business as you see it?

☐ What is the purpose of your business? What does it exist for?

☐ What are you trying to achieve? What are your aims and objectives?

☐ How do you measure your company's success?

☐ What are the biggest strengths, weaknesses, opportunities and threats to your business?

☐ If you had to give us some key things to remember so that we could do your job tomorrow, what would they be?

☐ Describe the competitive situation in the industry at the moment

☐ In what way do you expect the business to change in the future?

☐ What are the most critical factors in running this company?

General

☐ Can you give me an example of that?

☐ What happens when things go wrong?

☐ What would happen if you stopped doing 'xyz' activity?

☐ Take us through a typical day in your job

☐ What happens next, after 'xyz' activity?

Consolidation Checklist

Once the interview is over, perform consolidation as soon as possible:

☐ Inform the rest of the project team of key points from the interview

☐ Review notes for facts, opinions, issues, politics, etc.:
  - tidy up and make legible
  - highlight key concepts

☐ Update business models

☐ Add information and questions to the preparation for the next interview

☐ Inform or warn project team of politics, likes, dislikes, etc.

☐ Check that notes were labelled with:
  - date
  - time
  - place
  - interviewee
  - interviewer
  - note-taker
  - others present

☐ File notes for future reference

☐ Evaluate whether the goals for the interview have been met

☐ If not, what can be done about it? Note further questions that need to be asked

☐ Review interviewer and note-taker performance and identify areas for improvement.

Workshop and Feedback Checklist

Preparation of Models

The following lists have been used in many workshop and feedback sessions:

☐ Introduction and objectives overhead foils

☐ Business direction statements on overhead foils

★ ☐ Business-process models:

- overview foil for the process showing:
  ~ triggers
  ~ outcomes
  ~ cost/quality/time metrics
- build-up foils

★ ☐ Function hierarchy:

- foils for each function area in a file
- hard copy by each function area for each participant

★ ☐ Information model

- glossary for each participant
- one full model copy for session room
- entity-relationship build-ups by each function area in the function hierarchy file
- examples and questions for each function area
- one copy of the entity-diagram details for reference during the feedback.

★ optional for workshops

Handouts

☐ Title page

☐ Agenda

☐ Notebook or file folder to contain all handouts

☐ Glossary – appropriate reports from CASE tools

☐ Function hierarchy – appropriate reports from CASE tools

☐ Foil/ handout (one page) on how to read an entity model

☐ Pencil and paper.

Workshop and Feedback Environment

☐ Send reminder memorandum to participants

☐ Check that the room, or rooms if appropriate, have been booked

☐ Check that all equipment needed is available and **working**:

  – overhead projectors, with spare bulb (check it!)
  – overhead screens and pointer
  – ample overhead foils and cloth to wipe clean foils
  – projector pens, permanent or water based
  – computer with projection device, and spare bulb (check it!)
  – one flip chart for agenda, issues (for time management)
  – spare flip-chart paper
  – pens for flip chart
  – masking tape or similar (and permission) if you intend to stick completed sheeted on the wall
  – whiteboard and pens
  – memo stickers

☐ Food arrangements – organize:

  – water and glasses on table
  – morning coffee
  – lunch, as appropriate – this is **not** a heavy eating session
  – afternoon tea/coffee

☐ Seating arrangements – ensure that there are sufficient chairs, tables, etc. set out in advance with:

  – working-session table arrangement in an appropriate style – round, square, U-shaped
  – side tables as required
  – observers' seating
  – clear viewing, check for blind spots and hidden areas

☐ Ensure that any working sub-group rooms required are also equipped appropriately.

Supplies (reminder list)

☐ Pens for overhead projectors, flip charts and whiteboards

☐ Flip-chart paper

☐ Pointer

☐ Wipe cloth

☐ Blank overhead foils

☐ Memo stickers

☐ Paper and pencil.

Strategic Information Types

HINTS – use these to help you create questions for business analysis interviews. Although this list is quite extensive, it is by no means complete. You will want to add your own entries for the specific type of interview you are doing.

- ☐ Business direction – mission, objectives, strategy, key performance indicators, critical success factors
- ☐ External environment: key competitors, key customers, regulatory key suppliers
- ☐ Information required to do the task or job
- ☐ **What** is done, not how ... and **why** that is done ... instead of ...?
- ☐ Frequency function used
- ☐ Data volumes
- ☐ Seasonality
- ☐ Sequence of process/function
- ☐ Business unit associated with process/function
- ☐ Targets
- ☐ Financial indicators
- ☐ Volume of trade – annual (past, current and projected)
- ☐ Size of staff/manpower goals, turnover and training
- ☐ Age of company
- ☐ Organizational structure
- ☐ Product lines
- ☐ Projected growth – size, volume, revenue, etc.
- ☐ Portfolio of products
- ☐ Market share
    - by product
    - by region
    - over time
- ☐ Competitive position
    - by product
    - by product line
- ☐ Basis of forecasts (variables)
- ☐ Supplier links
- ☐ Economic factors – interest rates, inflation, trends

- ☐ Critical success factors for industry
- ☐ Size of company and branches
- ☐ Geographic location of all units of the company
- ☐ Productivity measures used – e.g. revenue per consultant, number of units manufactured per employee
- ☐ Types of variable costs and fixed costs, and cost to income ratio
- ☐ Debt management: debt to equity ratio compared with industry average
- ☐ Size of customer base
- ☐ Management of working capital – inventories and receivables
- ☐ Industry trends
- ☐ Fixed investment expressed as percentage of turnover and industry average
- ☐ Strategic issues – industry and company/competitive disadvantages
- ☐ Performance criteria
- ☐ Competitors' strategies and volumes
- ☐ Seasonality of business and cash-flow cycle
- ☐ Key SWOT – strengths, weaknesses, opportunities and threats
- ☐ Revenue per product, line and service
- ☐ Key customers.

GLOSSARY OF TERMS

This glossary contains a useful subset of the terms used in the CASE Method references and associated documents. Some of the words may not appear in this particular document, but they are included here for completeness and understanding.

Activity   In the context of the Business System Life Cycle, anything that needs to be done to complete a task. See **Task**.

Aim   See **Business Aim**.

Attribute   Any detail that serves to qualify, identify, classify, quantify or express the state of an entity.
or
Any description of 'a thing of significance'.

Note that each entity occurrence may only have one value of any attribute at one time.

Auditory Representational Style   A communication style characterized by the frequent use of words representing sounds or words seeking to elicit a verbal reply; for example, listen, harmonize, shout, say. See also **Verbal Matching**.

Body Language   Gestures and other non-verbal means by which feelings and intentions may be communicated; also known as non-verbal communication.

Briefing Session   A session held at the start of a project to inform participants of the purpose, schedule and roles in the project.

Build-up Foils   A sequence of overhead foils to build up a concept or a model from a simple starting point to a more complex end-point through a series of steps; useful in feedback sessions.

Business   An enterprise, commercial house or firm in either the private or public sector, concerned with providing products and/or services to satisfy customer requirements; for example, a car manufacturer, a refuse collection company, a legal advice provider, an organization providing health care.

Business Aim   A statement of business intent that may be measured subjectively; for example, to move up-market or to develop a sustainable level of growth. See also **Business Objective**.

Business Constraint   Any external, management or other factor that restricts a business or system development in terms of resource availability, dependencies, timescales or some other factor.

Business Direction Statement   A statement used to define the Mission, Aims, Business Strategies, Business Objectives, Critical Success Factors (CSF) or Key Performance Indicators (KPI) for an organization.

Business Function What a business or enterprise does or needs to do, irrespective of how it does it. See **Elementary Business Function**.

Business Interview A conversation held for the purpose of questioning and discovering the opinions or experience of another person.

Business Location A uniquely identifiable geographic location, site or place from which one or more business units may be wholly or partly operating.

Business Model A collection of models representing a definition of a business. Components include models of objectives, functions and information. See **Entity Relationship Diagram** and **Function Hierarchy**.

Business Objective A statement of business intent that may be measured quantifiably. A quantifiable goal or target. Aims and objectives are similar concepts but the achievement of an objective is measurable in some specific manner; for example, to increase profit by 10% during the next financial year.

Business Priority A statement of important business need or requirement within an ordered list.

Business Process A logical series of dependent activities that use the resources of the organization to create or result in an observable or measurable outcome, such as a product or service.

Business Process (Re-)Engineering The activity by which an enterprise re-examines its aims and how it achieves them, followed by the disciplined approach of redesigning how the business is carried out. Typically, this can also result in radically improved systems, which remove redundant activities, streamline and optimize resource utilization.

Business Strategy A plan of action that guides business decisions in a particular direction.

Business System Life Cycle A structured approach for the task of developing a business system. The seven major stages are strategy, analysis, design, build, documentation, transition and production. For interviewing purposes the cycle is condensed into three stages: strategy, analysis/design and implementation.

Business Unit Part of an organization which is treated for any purpose as a separate unit within the parent organization; for example, a department.

Business View A frequently used subset of information, readily intelligible to users and defined in business terms, derived from definitions held in an entity model. It is based on one entity and can encompass (renamed) attributes from this base entity and any other entity that is associated with it unambiguously.

Card Sorting A knowledge elicitation technique using cards; each card displays significant information such as an entity, object or rule and the cards are arranged and rearranged during a process to discover or confirm the relationships and associations between the items.

CASE Computer-Aided Systems Engineering is the combination of graphical, dictionary, generator, project management and other software tools to assist computer development staff engineer and maintain high-quality systems for their end users, within the framework of a structured method. It is also sometimes referred to as Computer-Aided Software Engineering.

CASE Method CASE Method is a structured approach to engineering systems in a data processing environment. It consists of a set of stages, tasks, deliverables and techniques, which lead you through all steps in the life cycle of a system. It is delivered via training courses, books and consultancy support, and can be automated by a combination of CASE tools.

CDE2 CASE Family A release of Oracle CASE business analysis and system development tools for PCs.

Closed Question A type of question that may be answered with a simple one or two word reply.

Company A commercial business.

Constraint See **Business Constraint**.

Contingency Planning Developing a plan for future actions depending upon possible conditions that may arise. A plan to answer 'what if...?'

Corporation A group of businesses acting as part of a single legal entity.

Consolidation A stage in the interview process where the material from an interview is reviewed, with extracts of key factors and key findings highlighted and summarized for future use; for example, extracting all potential entities for future modelling by circling nouns in an interview text.

Critical Case A special or rare situation. A description of this can give insight into the way things are done or decisions are made in normal situations.

Critical Success Factor Any business event, dependency, deliverable or other factor which, if not attained, would seriously impair the likelihood of achieving a business objective.

Database An arbitrary collection of tables or files under the control of a database management system.

Data Dictionary A repository for information recorded during a project.

Dataflow A named collection of entities, attributes, relationships and as yet unformalized information (data items) passing from one place to another, either between two steps in a business process or between a process step and a datastore or external entity. Dataflows may also be used with business functions. See **Business Function**, **Business Process** and **Datastore**.

Dataflow Diagram A diagram representing the use of data by business functions or steps in a business process. See **Dataflow** and **Datastore**.

Datastore A named collection of entities, attributes, relationships and as yet unformalized information (data items), as used by specified business functions or steps in a business process, which needs to be retained over a period of time. Storage may be temporary or permanent. During the early stage of analysis a datastore may contain data items, which are subsequently converted to attributes.

Decision Tree A graphic diagram logically representing the series of events and decisions related to decision making for one problem. The branches of a decision tree indicate the acts and events relating to the decision, thus alternative decisions are charted by different branches.

Delphi Technique A process used to elicit expert opinion and to obtain consensus between experts regarding a forecast or specific topic. In each round of the process, each expert provides one answer. This is recorded, ranked on a scale and anonymously reported to all participants, who then perform another round. The process continues until consensus is reached.

Domain A set of business validation rules, format constraints and other properties that apply to a group of attributes. For example:

- a list of values
- a range
- a qualified list or range
- any combination of these.

Note that attributes and columns in the same domain are subject to a common set of validation checks.

Domain (Expert) A topical area of knowledge; for example, a broad domain would be finance, a narrow domain would be analyzing a credit application.

Elementary Business Function A business function which, if started, must be completed successfully or, if for some reason it cannot be completed successfully, any changes it makes up to the point of failure must be undone, as though they had never happened. See **Function Hierarchy**.

End User The person for whom a system is being developed; for example, an airline reservations clerk is an end user of an airline reservations system.

Entity A thing of significance, whether real or imagined, about which information needs to be known or held. See **Attribute**.

Entity Relationship Diagram A part of the business model produced in the strategy stage of the Business System Life Cycle. The diagram pictorially represents entities, the vital business relationships between them and the attributes used to describe them. See **Entity, Attribute** and **Relationship**.

The process of creating this diagram is called entity modelling. The terms entity model, entity relationship model and entity/relationship model are all synonyms for Entity Relationship Diagram.

Event   A thing that happens or takes place, or an outcome or result: the arrival of a significant point in time, a change in status of something, or the occurrence of something external that causes the business to react. There are four types of event, all of which may act as triggers to one or more business functions.

Change Event – the status of something changes, and data is created or changed in such a manner as to act as a trigger for some business function(s); for example, when an entity is created or deleted, the value of an attribute is changed, or a relationship is connected or disconnected.

External Event – something happens outside the control of the business but is significant to the business in some way.

Time or Realtime Event – under specified conditions, real time reaches a predetermined date and time.

System Event – something significant within the control of the business occurs, such as completion of a particular function, and this acts as a trigger to initiate further functions.

Expert System   This encapsulates the expert knowledge of a human expert in a specific problem domain through symbolically encoding the knowledge in a specialized database and using logical procedures in a computer program to use the expert reasoning.

Facilitator   A role, one who directs a meeting or workshop using techniques to guide the process of the session to meet its aims and to aid in achieving full participation.

Feedback Session   A session held to obtain comments from a client group about work in progress such as models or plans.

Function   See **Business Function** and **Elementary Business Function**.

Function Decomposition   Any business function may be decomposed into lower levels of detail that are business functions themselves, and so on, until business functions that are atomic are reached. This function decomposition gives rise to functions arranged in groups/hierarchies known as a business function hierarchy.

Function Dependency   Often a function cannot commence until some condition has been fulfilled. Where this condition is the completion of another function there is a dependency between the two functions. Functions may also be dependent on events.

Function Dependency Diagram   A visual means of recording interdependencies between business functions, and showing events that cause functions to be triggered.

Function Hierarchy   A simple grouping of functions in a strict hierarchy, representing all the functions in an area of a business. This forms part of the business model produced in the strategy stage of the Business System Life Cycle. See **Business Function**.

Function Name   A short, succinct sentence, starting with a verb, describing what a business does or needs to do.

Groupware   Software enabling several persons in a group to simultaneously access the same computer-based material for the purpose of working on a mutual problem, plan or other joint decision making.

Hypothesis Testing   A confirmation technique whereby understanding of a subject is tested by making a statement (the hypothesis) and gaining another person's reaction to the accuracy of the statement.

Information Model   See **Entity Relationship Diagram**.

Information Systems   That part of an organization responsible for the development, operation and maintenance of computer-based systems. Also known as Information Technology, Information Systems Technology, Data Processing or I.T.

Interview   See **Business Interview**.

Interviewee Profile   A brief background of a person to be interviewed, giving insight into what the person is like, what he/she thinks is important, and areas of expertise and experience.

Key Performance Indicator   A measure used to evaluate the performance stated for a business objective; for example, number of days absent as a measure to evaluate the objective to reduce employee absenteeism by 10%.

Key Result   The outcome a business is trying to achieve upon receipt of an event. A key result is, in fact, simply an important event.

Kinaesthetic Representational Style   A communication style associated with the frequent use of words representing feelings of movements. See also **Verbal Matching**.

Knowledge Acquisition   The process of extracting the known facts, relationships and heuristics for a particular domain to be used in building an expert system.

Knowledge Elicitation   The techniques used for drawing out rules and domain knowledge from an expert.

Knowledge Engineer   The specialist role for the individual responsible for the assessment of problem domains, knowledge acquisition and the development of an expert system.

Lexical Analysis   Analysis of the words in a written text to extract key words, key elements (such as rules) and key principles for a given topic area. Also known as Text Analysis.

Mechanism   A particular technique or technology for implementing a function. Examples might be a telephone, a computer, an electronic mail service.

Mind Map   A diagram that is a network of connections, starting in the middle of the page with a key concept and radiating outwards – used for note-taking and to boost recall by linking related facts.

Mirroring   The act of adopting similar non-verbal signals between people; for example, similar body positions.

Mission Statement   A statement that communicates the purpose of the organization.

Module   A procedure that implements one or more business functions, or parts of business functions, within a computer system. Subsequently, a module will often be implemented by a computer program.

Non-Verbal Communication   See **Body Language**.

Objective   See **Business Objective**.

Open Question   A type of question that requires a full reply to complete the answer, rather than a simple one or two word reply.

Postural Echoing   See **Mirroring**.

Profile   See **Interviewee Profile**.

Program   A set of computer instructions, which can enter, change or query database items, and provide many useful computer functions.

Protocol Analysis   A knowledge elicitation technique using a written or video script created to describe each step taken by an expert to accomplish a specific goal.

Prototyping   A technique for demonstrating a concept rapidly, to gain acceptance and check feasibility. Within CASE Method use of a prototype is recommended during:

- Analysis – to check requirements and then be discarded.
- Design – to check feasibility of alternative options and to agree style (optionally discarding it).
- Build – to incrementally construct modules that need close user involvement.

Relationship   What one thing has to do with another.
or
Any significant way in which two things of the same or different type may be associated.

Note that it is important to name relationships.

Repertory Grid   A knowledge elicitation technique based on personal construct psychology methods. The basic method is to elicit attributes (descriptors) for an entity (subject) using a bipolar scale with the opposites for each attribute listed and ranked; for example, in describing location of services (subject) the attribute of expense is rated along a scale from inexpensive to expensive. The technique enables detailed examination of the subject.

Repository   A mechanism for storing any information to do with the definition of a system at any point in its life cycle. Repository services would typically be provided for extensibility, recovery, integrity, naming standards, and a wide variety of other management functions.

Representational Style   See **Auditory**, **Kinaesthetic** and **Visual Representational Styles**.

Reverse Engineering   An automatic and/or manual procedure that takes a component of an existing system and transforms it into a logical definition within a CASE tool.

Reverse engineering may apply to both data and computer programs. Such a logical definition so derived will often be refined, integrated with some new top-down definition of requirement, and forward engineered or generated to some replacement technology.

Scenario   A representative description of an imaginary situation; used to simulate the process of decision making used by an expert by means of a 'walk through' of the expert's reasoning process for solving the problem in that type of situation.

Scope   The subject matter to be covered by a project, often expressed in terms of the business process(es) to be examined or redesigned.

Semi-Structured Interview   An interview conducted according to a set of objectives and general checklist, but one without pre-set questions or topic sequence.

Stage   One of the seven major parts of the CASE*Method Business System Life Cycle.

Strategic Data Source   A source of business information that may cover a range of topics such as markets, technology, financial data, and so on, and may be global, national or for specific industries. Often available online through telecommunications links.

Storyboard   A technique, borrowed from the film industry, for describing screen dialogues. A storyboard consists of an ordered series of pictures, illustrating stages of the dialogue. The pictures are annotated with notes about logic and user input.

Structure Chart   A diagram that represents how a process or program may be designed in terms of actions and their sequence, choice and iteration.

Structured Interview   An interview conducted strictly according to a set, predetermined plan including a full text for all questions written in advance.

Sub-type   A type of entity. An entity may be split into two or more sub-types, each of which has common attributes and/or relationships. These are defined explicitly once only at the higher level. Sub-types may have attributes and/or relationships in their own right. A sub-type may be further sub-typed to lower levels.

SWOT Analysis   A structured way of thinking about and analyzing strengths, weaknesses, opportunities and threats.

Synonym   A word or phrase with the same meaning as another (in a given context); for example, aircraft and aeroplane.

System   A named, defined and interacting collection of real-world facts, procedures and processes, along with the organized deployment of people, machines, various mechanisms and other resources that carry out those procedures and processes.

In a good system the real-world facts, procedures and processes are used to achieve their defined business purposes with acceptable tolerances.

Task   A task is the first subdivision of a stage. See **Stage**.

Text Analysis   See **Lexical Analysis**.

Twenty Questions   A knowledge elicitation technique; an expert asks twenty questions, which lead to a decision on a subject; for example, questions regarding symptoms for the medical diagnosis of a given disease.

Unique Identifier   Any combination of attributes and/or relationships that serves, in all cases, to uniquely identify an occurrence of an entity.
or
Any combination of columns that serves, in all cases, to uniquely identify an occurrence of a row in a table.

Primary keys and unique indexes are alternative ways of implementing unique identifiers on a relational database management system.

Unstructured Interview   An interview conducted in a 'free association' style and without any preparation or pre-set questions.

User   Any person or group of people with some rights to access a computer facility. The same person may be known to a sophisticated system in several ways; for example, as a database user, CASE user, user of an operating system, package user, user of an electronic mail system, and so on.

Verbal Matching   The ability to modify the words and phrases used in speech to match the representational style of an interviewee. See **Auditory**, **Kinaesthetic** and **Visual Representational Styles**.

Visual Representational Style   A communication style associated with the frequent use of words representing visual imagery or words to elicit graphics, diagrams or other visual examples. Also see **Verbal Matching**.

Workshop   A meeting for concerted activity; a working session designed for active participation in focused tasks by all those present.

Workflow   The sequence of activities required to carry out some task. See also **Business Process**.

Wrap-up Questions   Questions towards the end of an interview that give the interviewee a chance to discuss topics not covered already.

Index

Where a given term has several references, primary references are highlighted in bold. An index entry starting with the letters **Ch** references an entire chapter. A single letter entry references an entire appendix.